READY TO HEAL

Women Facing Love, Sex, and Relationship Addiction

Kelly McDaniel

GENTLE PATH PRESS
P.O. BOX 3172
Carefree, AZ 85377
www.gentlepath.com
800-708-1796

First Printing, February 2008

Production Manager: Suzanne O'Connor
Editor: Amy Campbell
Graphic Design: Adam Wheat
Cover Design: Adam Wheat

Gentle Path

P   R   E   S   S

GENTLE PATH PRESS
P.O. BOX 3172
Carefree, AZ 85377
www.gentlepath.com
800-708-1796

Contents

Ready to Heal

When love hurts, you may wonder about your romantic choices or difficulty with sexuality. Perhaps, like many others, you are experiencing the pain of an addictive relationship–the kind of relationship that's painful to be in, yet impossible to leave. Living with this kind of relationship brings a profound sense of emptiness. You feel pain, anger and confusion rather than much desired closeness, warmth and security. You find yourself feeling broken.

As a woman, you are wired for relationships. However, when relationships become a "drug," you're in a painful paradox. The intimacy you need and want becomes distant. The more you try, the deeper you sink in the quicksand of despair.

The idea of love or sex being a drug may be new to you. It could sound unlikely. You may even be recovering from other addictions and find there is another layer of addictive behavior yet to address. Or perhaps you've considered for some time that your relationships could be addictive. When love and sex become addictive, a certain person or relational pattern becomes all-consuming. Your well-being hinges on this particular pattern or person rather than a spiritual serenity within.

The concept of being addicted to love or sex is not new. Women who "love too much" have been the subject of writing and talk shows for decades. However, new research illuminates the complicated nature of relationship addiction. Thanks to the writing and research of Dr. Patrick Carnes most professionals no longer debate whether or not the addiction is real. In the field of relationship addiction, women are typically divided in two categories. You are considered a "co-addict" if you're in a relationship with a sex addict, or a "sex addict" if you have patterns of destructive, promiscuous behavior.

While these compartments can be helpful in the initial stages of identifying an addiction, the distinctions often serve to separate women from one another. Women who suffer with love, sex or relationship addiction are already isolated from other women. When you decide to face this disease, you will need friendships with women in order to heal. Therefore, the differences between co-addict and addict are less important than the marked similarities. Recovering from addictive relationships requires *accepting that you in fact have an addiction to a distinct relational pattern.* The specifics of *how* you are addicted to love or sex are less important than the fact that you are, and you're not alone.

I get asked this question quite regularly: "Are only beautiful women addicted to sex?" The question illustrates the grave misunderstanding of this disease. Sex and love addiction is not about being beautiful. It's not even about enjoying sex. Sex and love addiction, like any other addiction, is about pain, shame, and control. Most women, in addictive relationships report using sex to please a partner or separating from their body during a sexual encounter. Many fake the enjoyment of sex. Women who discuss enjoying sex focus on the power, control and energy that comes from being wanted. This is very different from actually enjoying a sensual, intimate sexual experience that involves trust and mutuality. Most women struggling in addictive relationships have never known this kind of experience.

You will notice in this book a distinct absence of descriptive details when it comes to the stories women have shared. There is no mention of beauty, hair color, skin tone, or clothing. Typically, case studies include these kinds of details. In a book about addictive sex and love, however, these details become problematic. They serve to titillate or separate. Neither fosters healing. Therefore, I have chosen to omit physical attributes from the stories women have shared with me. My hope is that rather than focus on how a woman looks, the focus will be on how she feels, how she faces this disease, and how she heals.

While identities have been altered for privacy purposes, the stories contain universal themes that may help you identify patterns in your own life. Undoubtedly, there will be pieces of your life that are not represented here. You are unique in your relational patterns and addictive tendencies. The way your romantic history plays out will not be identical to someone else's. However, you may find common beliefs and similar behavior when you explore the stories in this book.

Most of the stories are from heterosexual women. A separate book for lesbians is critical. Although many of the issues are universal for lesbians and heterosexual women, the shame that lesbians encounter when exploring sexual issues can be more complicated than for heterosexual women. While both heterosexual and homosexual women face self-hatred that comes from our cultural inheritance, heterosexual women do not encounter homophobia when they address this disease.

I invite you to explore the stories in this book with a kind heart. Be curious about how sex, romance or love becomes addictive. As you read Chapters Two and Three on culture and family abuse, examine your own upbringing. In Chapters Four and Five, identify patterns of behavior that are part of your addictive cycle. Chapter Six will challenge you to reflect about ways your body tells your story. And Chapters Seven, Eight, and Nine ask you to wonder about the recovery process and what it could mean for your life. If at any point, you feel overloaded or triggered by what you read, stop and take a break. This material can be difficult to assimilate.

Facing this addiction requires compassion, awareness and willingness as you explore the unknown. However, there are unexpected gifts in store for you when you face love and sex addiction. Part of the addiction is a desperate longing to be loved. Since love, connection, and sexual intimacy are basic human needs, healing their distortions naturally put you in a place to receive them. Your efforts to heal prepare you to give and receive love in healthy ways rather than addictive, painful ways. Part of being ready to heal is having faith that although you don't know what will happen, you move forward anyway, embracing the journey toward relational and sexual health.

Chapter One
Sex and Love Addiction

"David was catnip and kryptonite to me."
Elizabeth Gilbert, *Eat, Pray, Love*

David and I had broken up for good. Or maybe we hadn't. It's hard to remember how many times we broke up and joined up over those months. But there emerged a pattern: I would separate from David, get my strength and confidence back, and then (attracted as always by my strength and confidence) his passion for me would rekindle. Respectfully, soberly and intelligently, we would discuss "trying again" always with some sane new plan for minimizing our apparent incompatibilities. We were so committed to solving this thing. Because how could two people who were so in love not end up happily ever after? It had to work. Didn't it? Reunited with fresh hopes, we'd share a few deliriously happy days together. Or sometimes even weeks. But eventually David would retreat from me once more and I would cling to him (or I would cling to him and he would retreat—we never could figure out how it got triggered) and I'd end up destroyed all over again. And he'd end up gone.[1]

Elizabeth Gilbert's description of her romance with David captures the exquisite torture of an addictive relationship. Many women find themselves in an addictive relationship at one time or another. For some women, however, addictive relationships are the norm. Their relationships have patterns of extreme highs and lows that are intoxicating, but eventually draining.

Some women find themselves compulsively attached to one relationship and unable to separate even when the circumstances clearly warrant such a measure. Other women may find themselves seeking "the perfect" partner, moving from relationship to relationship, without an ability to commit more than a few months to each one. In some cases, a woman closes off her sexual self in an effort to stay safe and feel invulnerable. The women in this book have one thing in common: Their romantic lives aren't satisfying, and the steady presence of isolation is causing terrible pain.

Perhaps you too have experienced the pain of an addictive relationship–the kind of relationship that's painful to be in, yet impossible to leave. You probably felt confused, alone, and angry. At times, you thought you were the problem. The relationship may have been chaotic or boring. Either way you're familiar with loneliness and confusion. Loneliness can be a difficult emotion to identify. For women, feeling lonely brings terrible shame.

For this reason, loneliness often masquerades as confusion. You might feel lost, disoriented, and unable to identify why relationships hurt so badly. One client explained loneliness like this:

...if I'm addicted to men, that's one thing. But if it's because I'm lonely, that's not OK. It means I must be a total loser.

She's articulating what many women feel: "If I'm lonely, it must be my fault...there must be something wrong with me."

Women in Pain

Addictive relationship patterns take many forms. Some women find themselves compulsively drawn to partners who have an addiction to sex. In these relationships a woman may be identified as a "co-addict." Other women find they are struggling with their own romance or sexual addiction using sex to feel loved or powerful. Sometimes a woman does both. Painful romantic patterns take many forms and rarely does a woman demonstrate only one pattern.

For example, Maria, who you will meet later in this chapter, learned to get attention by being flirtatious and overtly sexual. However, in her marriage she completely shut down sexually and lost all desire for physical contact with her husband. Maria had difficulty seeking treatment for her romantic patterns because she didn't have a name for her behavior. One male therapist tried to seduce her; another pushed her to be sexual with her husband. No one seemed to understand the nature of her disease. For many women like Maria, therapy can be a frustrating experience. Most therapists aren't trained to handle the complex nature of addictive relationships. Consider the following:

Brooklyn

Brooklyn, a woman in her mid-thirties, met the "man of her dreams" four years ago when they were in rehab for drug addiction. Brooklyn and Ray ignored the treatment center's guidelines to avoid romantic relationships for at least a year and quickly got married. Now the relationship isn't working. Brooklyn feels rage toward her husband. She doesn't feel he gives her enough attention, and their sexual relationship isn't satisfying her. She started an affair with a former lover, and although her husband knows nothing of the affair, the tension in their household is building. Brooklyn is living two lives. She doesn't understand how she can juggle this behavior, yet she has no intention of stopping saying, "I don't feel guilty."

Brooklyn's story is an example of how a woman can use sex to gain a sense of power in her relationship. Her affair hides her true feelings. She can't be vulnerable with her husband as long as she is medicating her loneliness with another lover. Brooklyn uses sex outside the marriage for the attention she craves.

In early recovery, a newly sober person can be very needy and dependent. Brooklyn mistook her husband's neediness as a sign of love. Neediness is intense and can look like passionate adoration. As the marriage unfolded, however, and the truth of his emotional unavailability became apparent, Brooklyn felt betrayed and justified in her attempts to find sexual attention outside her marriage. Her pursuit of attention covered up the painful reality that deep inside she too felt needy and dependent. Like her husband, Brooklyn is unavailable for intimacy because she has not yet had time to heal the wounds underneath her need for an addiction.

Susan

Susan just completed graduate school and has an MS in social work. She is seeing a therapist because she's in a destructive relationship that she can't get out of. She has tried to break up with her boyfriend numerous times, but always returns. He is an artist who makes a living teaching art classes and selling paintings, but he's also an alcoholic. His alcohol use comes in spurts, and Susan never knows what to expect when he starts to drink. Although he's successful around town and she enjoys accompanying him to his art shows, she becomes more frightened the longer she's with him.

Sometimes when they argue he becomes violent. Recently he left her at a restaurant during an argument, taking the car and her house keys with him. It was late and she didn't feel safe going home. She called a friend to come get her, which left her feeling truly embarrassed. Before this incident, she had managed to keep the frightening nature of her relationship a secret. Now, asking for help, she felt exposed and ashamed. She had no answers for her friend's concerned questions about the relationship. Susan has one more secret. She recently discovered she was pregnant and had an abortion. She didn't feel safe having a child with her lover. Susan is acting outside her value system, but can't get away and doesn't know why.

Susan is caught in a trauma bond. Trauma bonds are relationships that look unhealthy to friends or family, but the two individuals involved can't break the destructive patterns. They are caught in a cycle of fear and arousal that's intense and addictive. Women from all ethnicities, socio-economic backgrounds, and education levels find themselves in trauma bonds. It has nothing to do with intelligence. The bond is a replay of childhood wounding that has never healed. Traumatic relationships are a way to self-abuse. A woman can use a destructive relationship to destroy her health and her life. In Chapter Six, we'll explore trauma bonds in more depth.

Evelyn

Evelyn is fifty-six and has been married five times. She's currently divorced and works as a salesperson for an electronics company. Evelyn drinks every day after work and occasionally takes pain pills to alter her moods. She's sought treatment with many therapists, but each time she finds a new lover she quits therapy, returning only when things become painful again. She has trouble sleeping, waking three or four times a night. She can't figure out what is wrong. Although she doesn't have a boyfriend or a husband, she's meeting men online and having casual sex.

Evelyn is showing signs of sex addiction. Sex, like pain pills, can be used to alter unpleasant feelings or moods. Sex creates a high, and the pursuit of a new lover can take up time that otherwise might be spent feeling sad and depressed. In Evelyn's case, she's avoiding something painful. Her efforts to numb herself are failing, however, as she finds herself waking often at night plagued with horrible feelings of panic and restlessness. She has been in therapy many times, but each time she finds a new boyfriend, she abandons the healing process. Progress in therapy often brings pain. Pain comes before there is the reward of awareness and change. Like many women, Evelyn prefers an immediate escape from her pain through drugs and sex.

Painful Patterns

Research shows that women develop self-awareness and understanding in relationships, not separate from them. Therefore, women need relationships. In addictive relationships, however, women experience chronic pain and psychological isolation. When a woman is noticing disturbing relational patterns she may find some of the following to be true.

- She is not at "ease" or at peace.
- She never knows a moment of comfort in solitude.
- She has an inability to be alone or be still.
- She often has disordered eating patterns, sleep patterns, and/or financial patterns.
- She will grow increasingly confused and tired.
- She won't trust people.
- She will grow increasingly isolated while pursuing sex or romance.
- She will lose interest in friends, hobbies, family, and work.
- She will not live within her value system or she may not have a value system.
- She will have increasing episodes of irritability, rage, and restlessness.

Maria described her romantic patterns in the following way:

I was convinced that being myself would never get me love and attention, so I became a desperate people-pleaser and did everything I could to be whatever anyone else wanted me to be. The more attention I got, the more I wanted. I was caught in a bind because even when I succeeded in getting attention, I didn't trust it. So I craved more reassurance and grew more needy. I pushed away the very thing I needed and I didn't know how to do anything else.

Painful romantic patterns have their roots in early abuse experiences and damaging cultural beliefs. When female development is distorted, adult relationships take on characteristics of codependency and addiction. Codependency is a widely used term with many definitions. In this book, codependency is understood to be the unmet developmental needs that fuel the need for compulsive behavior. When age-appropriate needs for attachment, safety, and bonding are not met, a woman develops desperate and compulsive behavior to meet her valid need for connection.

In this way, examining addictive use of sex or love cannot be separated from an understanding of codependency. Codependency, like an addiction, is an attempt to control reality (or another person) in an effort to avoid painful feelings. Codependency breeds compulsive behavior. In fact, some understand codependency AS compulsive behavior. In this way, codependency and addictive relationships are intertwined for women and the differences become less clear.

Women who become addicted to relationships and sex are escaping not only painful feelings, but the painful cultural inheritance that places them in an inferior position to men. Sexual power can turn the tables. Instead of feeling weak or inferior in a relationship, women learn to use sex to dominate, seduce, control, or maintain romantic relationships.

When relationships become addictive, love is a struggle for power rather than an experience of intimacy. Painful patterns of thinking dominate the romantic experience. There are four distorted ways of thinking in addictive relationships.

Secrecy is better than honesty. In many families, children grow up learning to protect family secrets. Certain issues are kept behind closed doors. Families adopt a "don't talk" rule about these painful issues, and as a result, a child internalizes the need for secrets. She learns that honesty is dangerous. If she speaks about certain issues or emotions, she risks anger and alienation from her family. Therefore, as an adult, she finds herself automatically telling lies, keeping secrets, and being dishonest. Secrecy kills intimacy.

I can't be angry and be loved. Children learn to hide anger or express it indirectly. As adults, the inability to feel and share anger damages intimacy. Anger is a normal part of being alive and being in a relationship. When it's denied, it has the power to destroy the potential for authentic intimacy between two people.

Compromise means loss of power. In families where an authority figure dominates the household, compromise doesn't exist. Children learn that there is only one way to be right, and being right is the most important thing. They also learned to sacrifice their own needs and desires to please the authority figure.

As a result, when they are adults they hunger for control and have many unmet needs. In relationships, it feels more important to be right than to find mutually agreeable solutions that require giving up something desirable. It's more important to win, because in the unconscious mind losing represents a total loss of self.

People will always leave me and can't be trusted. Adults who find themselves repeatedly in addictive relationships have a profound fear of abandonment. Abandonment fear can masquerade two ways: extreme dependency or fear of suffocation. Dependency can appear desperate or empty. A woman feels a frightening void when she's alone, which she avoids with constant activity or romance. In the case of suffocation, a woman will feel if she lets her guard down she will be used and smothered. She builds emotional walls to keep her at a safe distance from others.

A Need for a Name

To begin healing addictive romantic patterns, it's necessary to first have a name for the problem. Naming this particular problem, however, is complicated. Women have been called many names for their sexual and romantic choices. If a woman enjoys her sexuality, she's labeled "promiscuous," "whore," or "slut." On the flip side, if a woman shows a lack of sexual desire, she's called "frigid" or "cold." How do women reconcile these two extremes? Oftentimes, we find that there is no possible way for a woman to experience her sexuality without the experience of shame. Shame is the result of an impossible impasse between two rules. *There is a very narrow cultural margin within which a woman can define her sexual choices.*

This margin contributes to a cultural belief system that, as a woman, *I will never be enough and I will never be worthy of love.* In the words of Dr. Christiane Northrup, author of *Women's Bodies, Women's Wisdom,* "Our culture gives girls and women the message that their bodies, their lives, and their femaleness demand an apology."[2] Sexual shame is a terrible cultural inheritance for women. So by exploring dysfunctional sexual patterns, there's a risk that you may feel shame as you read these chapters and stories. Be gentle with yourself as you think about your sexual life and romantic choices.

Jane, a client in her late thirties, explains the relief she felt when she learned there was a name for what she was doing.

I just thought I was broken, that something was wrong with me. I had no idea there was a name for what I was doing romantically, and that there might be a way to change. I desperately did not want to continue hurting others or myself, but felt that it was just my personality.

Naming the dis-ease of sex and love addiction

Disease is understood as a state of being ill at ease or a disruption in normal functioning. In this way, we can understand how sex and romance can become a disease. Relationships can inhibit your normal functioning. They can take over your life. When a woman is not at ease, or in dis-ease with her sexual and romantic life, she suffers. If you have had the experience of disregarding your truth, your obligations, or your health in order to pursue a romantic situation, you know this kind of dis-ease.

Perhaps you've experienced the distorted thinking (mentioned before) that thrives in addictive relationships. Distorted thinking is painful, and grows in strength at times making you feel crazy. Disease thrives in distortion.

Northrup explains that in order to heal dis-ease and promote positive change in your life, you must first name your experience. A name provides energy and direction for the healing process to begin. While considering a name for this dis-ease, it's helpful to understand a working definition of addiction. For the purposes of this book, we will use the following definition: addiction is a "pathological relationship with a mood-altering substance or experience." To understand addiction in this way is to see addiction as a relationship. A person enters into relationship with a substance or experience.

Stephanie Covington, Ph.D., and Janet Surrey, Ph.D., find that the addiction "is a kind of love relationship in which the object of addiction becomes the focus of a woman's life." [3] For an alcoholic, alcohol becomes the love object. With food addiction, food becomes a best friend. With an addiction, the substance becomes the focus of a woman's energy and time. Progressively, more of her life belongs to this "relationship." Consider, then, how confusing it can be when romance is the "love object." In essence, her "love" relationship becomes her addiction.

Initially, the mood-altering experience of falling in love or being sexual feels warm, safe, and inviting. In the early stages, there is a feeling of euphoria and bliss. A woman experiences increased energy, clarity, and joy when falling in love. She's happy. So how could it be a problem if all these great feelings become an addiction? Can too much of a good thing become bad? In the popular lyrics of Fleetwood Mac, "I'm over my head…but it sure feels nice." Or Diana Ross' "If there's a cure for this…I don't want it!"

Romantic bliss seems to be what makes life worth living. Yet for many women, there's a dark side to the search for intimacy and connection. Romance addiction twists relationships into a mechanism for pain. Love and sex become distorted and the relationships that used to bring you joy and pleasure now bring pain and despair. Over and over again, relationships fail. Some days you feel broken. You wonder how you got here. You may try to recreate a particular relationship to feel good again. But unfortunately, nothing you try works for very long.

Many Names for the Same Disease

While professionals agree on the definition for addiction, therapists and authors have difficulty defining an addiction to sex and love with any uniformity. This is due, in part, to the resistance that pursuit for love or sex could become addictive. In a culture "in love" with love, it's understandable that this is an unpopular idea. A number of specialists treating addiction and women, however, have successfully formed categories to help women understand their painful romantic patterns.

In *Escape From Intimacy,* author Anne Wilson Shaef outlines three categories: romance addiction, relationship addiction and sexual addiction.[4] They are defined as:

Romance Addiction

A romance addict is someone who gets a "buzz" or a fix from "love" and romance. The romance addict is an expert in illusion, and believes the fantasy that "someday my prince will come." The romance addict enjoys candlelight dinners, weekends away, and planning for a romantic "experience." Sometimes the person is not important; it's the experience of romance that "hooks" the romance addict.

The character Charlotte in the popular HBO series *Sex and the City* is a perfect example of a romance addict. Charlotte loves romance and fancy dinners. She wants her partner to wear the right clothes, live in the right place, and attend the right social occasions. After years of dating, she finally meets her handsome "prince," the man with the right education, career, and income. Her romantic fantasies are finally fulfilled, except her perfect prince cannot consummate the marriage. Instead, he masturbates to porn in the bathroom while she's asleep. Rather than finding her true prince in her pursuit of the perfect romance, Charlotte has married a sex addict, a man completely unable to be sexual with anything more than a magazine image of a woman.

Relationship Addiction

Relationship addicts fall into two categories: those addicted to the "idea" of a relationship, any relationship; and those who are addicted to one particular relationship or person. Shaef explains that relationship addicts do not really have relationships, rather "they have hostages."[5]

Sexual Addiction

Sexual addiction is an obsession and preoccupation with sex, in which everything "is defined sexually or by its sexuality and all perceptions and relationships are sexualized."[6] For a woman addicted to sex, sex is a goal. It's the highlight of a relational experience. However, few women are addicted to sex without a relationship. And as a result, codependency and sexual addiction often coexist, making a separate diagnosis of sexual addiction limiting for women.

Shaef observes that sex is a "hidden addiction."[7] While more women are beginning to question their sexual behavior, the shame that surrounds sexuality often inhibits deeper exploration. Many women have difficulty with the concept that their sexuality could be addictive. This is understandable. Sex addiction seems to be reserved for men. Images of male sex addicts are often frightening, perverted, or exploited by the media, making the concept of sexual addiction something to be feared. Sex addiction, therefore, carries shame. For this reason, the categories "romance and relationship" addiction permit a reduced threat to a woman identifying painful romantic patterns that often include compulsive sexuality.

Notice that "love" addiction doesn't appear in the three categories. According to Shaef,

... no interpersonal or pseudo-relationship addiction has anything to do with love. These addictions may have something to do with the illusion of love, and they have nothing to do with true loving ...[7]

This is a very important distinction. Addiction, in fact, is not love. However, for many women, the difference between love and addiction isn't clear. So using the word love to describe addictive behavior may be appropriate. Women can identify with love being addictive more easily than sex. Truthfully, the brain doesn't really care. It doesn't distinguish between sex and love. Both love and sex produce wonderful hormones that feel good.

In *Facing Love Addiction,* author Pia Melody uses "love addiction" to describe the disease in all its forms. Melody describes a love addict as a person who turns

... to another person and to compulsive behavior within a relationship (this could include sex) as a drug of choice for removing the pain of the difficulties in their relationship with themselves...[8]

Melody explains that

... those who are compulsively driven to try to get someone else to tell them that they are lovable and loved are termed Love Addicts...the obsession about the other party, constantly thinking about the person, wanting to be with him or her, to make contact emotionally, physically, every way possible, is part of love addiction.[9]

For many women, these words describe every experience they've had in relationships. These words describe what many women experience as love. Women find themselves both addicted to relationships or to certain behavior patterns in the relationship. A woman uses compulsive behavior to change herself and maintain the illusion of love. Compulsive romantic behavior increases in intensity over time. The following list of compulsive behaviors may help you identify some of the ways you've tried to preserve the illusion that you're in love or in a healthy relationship.

- checking a partner's e-mail without telling him/her
- checking a partner's paper correspondence, alcohol usage, drug intake, etc.
- looking at women or men the partner may be seeing
- changing the way you dress or wear makeup to please a partner

- changing friends and hobbies to please a partner
- checking a partner's cell phone without permission
- trying to figure out what a partner is thinking
- obsessing about where and what a partner is doing
- neglecting self-care while in relationship with a partner
- searching for sexual attention outside a primary relationship (including Internet activity of an emotional or sexual nature)
- compulsive use of food, money, alcohol, drugs, and/or sex to avoid intimacy

Although Melody uses the term "love addiction," it's clear that she isn't referring to authentic love. She's describing the illusion of love. Love addiction is dependency, neediness, and control, not love. Understood in this way, Melody's love addict is similar to Shaef's romance or relationship addict. Many love addicts use sex to keep their relationship, and over time find themselves addicted to sexual intensity. In this manner, Melody's love addict could also be Shaef's sex addict.

In trying to find a working name for this particular addiction, we turn to the St. Augustine Fellowship, a 12-step program designed for men and women addicted to sex and love. Sex and Love Addicts Anonymous (SLAA) originated in Boston in December 1976. The St. Augustine Fellowship sums up the reality of sex and love addiction in the following words:

... those who found that a basic human need for close relationship with one another, combined with a realization of one's sexual capacities as an expression of commitment in such a relationship, could be debased by addiction into a compulsive search for sex and romance, or obsessional entrapment in relationships characterized by personal neediness and hyperdependency–in patterns that could forever prevent really meeting the underlying need for authentic experience of self and other.[10]

The St. Augustine definition of romance addiction adequately encompasses the pain of the disease: *the lost opportunity for a true authentic experience of intimacy.* The name "sex and love addiction" has room for all the variations of this addiction. It includes romance addiction, relationship addiction, co-addiction (addicted to a sex addict), love addiction, and sex addiction.

You may find you identify more with one of the other names we have mentioned. The important issue is that you find a name that fits you. Regardless of how your painful patterns of love and sex manifest, the term sex and love addiction holds room for each form of the disease. The different ways of naming this addiction becomes less important than the truth: addictive relational patterns involving love and sex are painful and can become life threatening.

Codependency, Power, and Sex

In the following pages you'll read stories about real women who discovered they have an addiction to love and sex. We'll follow the development of the disease in each of these women and others throughout the book. At this point, you may notice some common themes that develop in each woman's story. While there's no exact recipe that can predict if a woman will become a sex and love addict, there are certain environments that seem to breed the disease:

- a cultural environment that places women in an inferior position to men and objectifies their sexuality
- a family environment that creates psychological isolation
- a parent or parents who are in an addictive relationship(s)
- a primary female caregiver who is unavailable for healthy bonding and role modeling
- a primary male caregiver who is unpredictable, at times creating fear and/or sexual intensity
- sex and fear are part of the home atmosphere

Maria

Maria is the firstborn daughter of a middle-class Hispanic family where her parents filled traditional gender roles. Her father worked and her mother stayed home to raise the children. They were active members in their Catholic church and community. Maria has few happy memories of her childhood. She remembers being mostly afraid. When her father wasn't working, he was home, sullen, and angry. His moods terrified Maria as she never knew what to expect from him. He physically punished her regularly, and although spanking was considered normal in the late '60s and early '70s, it's now understood to be a form of physical abuse. The spankings Maria endured were extraordinary. Her father removed her clothing and spanked her until she screamed and sobbed.

Her mother was also unhappy in the marriage and in their home. She was critical, unpredictable, and rarely affectionate. Maria had four sisters, all very close in age, and the girls often took refuge in one another as they couldn't rely on their mother for comfort. Maria loved her younger sisters and recalls feelings of rage and terror when her sisters were beaten by their father. She desperately wanted to protect them but was powerless to do so. As a grown woman, her sisters' screams still echo in her mind. This is a good example of how the beating of a sibling can be traumatizing for the other sibling(s) to witness.

As a young child Maria found ways to comfort herself. She enjoyed Disney stories and longed to be beautiful like Snow White and Cinderella so that some day she would be rescued from her misery. Her fantasy life carried her through the lonely nights at home. Maria masturbated every day as a young girl, although she doesn't remember how she learned. Her mother caught her once and screamed at her. She told Maria that masturbation was a sin and that she would not be able to have a husband if she continued. Although this scared Maria, she couldn't stop masturbating. It was her only comfort. She just tried harder to be secretive.

As a child, Maria unknowingly learned how to alter her struggling brain chemistry with orgasm. (We will examine abuse and brain chemistry in Chapters Three and Six). The feel-good hormones released during masturbation soothed Maria's fear and loneliness. For children, masturbation and food are two of the most accessible ways to alter brain chemistry in an effort to feel better. If a child is not able to attach to her caregivers, she will find something to attach to. In Maria's case, fantasy and masturbation provided a solace from the horrible isolation and pain of her childhood.

As an adolescent, Maria showed symptoms of post-traumatic stress disorder (PTSD). Although she was a good student, she had trouble concentrating on school work. Her attention span was short and she had difficulty being still or quiet. She remembers always holding her breathe. She had frequent stomach problems and remembers suffering at school. She dreaded going home but did not feel safe at school either. Maria also experienced regular nightmares throughout her childhood. Today, these symptoms may be diagnosed as attention deficit disorder (ADD) or attention deficit hyperactivity disorder (ADHD). Oftentimes, trauma is overlooked as a possible reason a child may be having difficulty in school or with peers.

Maria experienced her first taste of sexual pleasure in the fifth grade when her friend Travis kissed her in a dark closet. Maria describes the kiss like an alcoholic describes a first drink.

It was dark. I couldn't see but somehow I knew I was about to be kissed. I was shocked when his tongue touched my mouth and opened my lips. He was so soft and gentle and I had butterflies in my stomach. I felt euphoric, and I thought that I would always need Travis to be happy.

Travis and Maria explored each other's bodies often, but always secretively. At school, Travis wouldn't acknowledge her. While Maria adored his attention, deep inside, she was hurt and angry. This went on with Travis for three years until Maria, at fourteen, fell in love with someone new. She recalls immediately "turning off" feelings for Travis, channeling all her energy into the new boy, Matt.

With Matt, Maria did anything to please him, just as she had with Travis. She held Matt on a pedestal. She admired his intelligence, athletic ability, and the fact that he was older. She laughed at all his jokes and thought about him all the time. They began a sexual relationship, but Maria refused to have intercourse. Her Catholic upbringing and parents' rules made her fear she would go to Hell if she had premarital intercourse.

So Matt taught her how to give oral sex, and he expected it any time he took her to dinner, a movie, or even to run an errand. He wanted oral sex all the time.

Maria hated it, but never refused. In fact, she recalls learning how to swallow so that she wouldn't taste his ejaculate.

Maria's lack of attachment with her parents set her up for painful codependency. Her family relationships didn't provide her a safe place to bond or to form an identity. As a result, she was vulnerable and needed outside validation to feel worthwhile and loved. Sexual attention from boys felt like love. Her early fantasy life programmed her to think sexual attention from boys might be love. Even though she didn't like sex, she needed the relationship to feel worthwhile. So she used sex as a means to feel loved.

Grateful for Matt's attention, Maria masked her confusion and shame about her sexual behavior for two years. But she felt different. She felt dirty. At school, she was student council president, a member of the school drama club, and a "good" girl. But when she was with Matt, she felt secretive, lonely, and "bad." None of her peers seemed to share her need for sexual attention. Her shame and anger began to grow.

When she was seventeen, she suddenly "fell out of love" with Matt and found a new boyfriend. Again she turned off feelings just like she had done before. This relationship, however, was different, requiring Maria's codependency to evolve. Her new boyfriend didn't want to have sex, which confused and frustrated Maria. She was programmed to be sexual. She didn't know how to behave romantically without sexual intensity so she ended the relationship.

In college, Maria's need for male attention escalated. She craved attention from men, but never trusted it. She alienated men early in the relationships with her flirtatious behavior that could be directed at any guy at any time. She also had unpredictable mood swings. Maria was still hanging onto her virginity, but growing increasingly reckless with her emotional and sexual behavior. By her sophomore year, she was alone and suicidal, depressed, overweight, drinking too much, and failing in one relationship after another. Maria's out-of-control sexual behavior made her reckless.

One night she left a bar with a stranger and was raped. Her shame kept her quiet, and she blamed herself because she had willingly put herself at risk. When she called her mother to talk about her suicidal feelings, her mother's lack of interest drove her further into isolation.

Since she had lost her virginity, Maria decided to have sexual intercourse without worrying about the religious consequences. She began a sexual relationship with a man named Lee who didn't attend her school, hoping to keep her sexual life separate from her college life. She also chose Lee because he was her friend. She wasn't particularly attracted to him, so she felt less vulnerable. She felt safe. She knew he needed her and this gave her a sense of power. Maria had been powerless as a child and in her other relationships. With Lee, she felt strong, independent, and sexual. But she didn't love or respect him. As she approached her senior year of college, Maria panicked and decided to find someone she could marry.

She broke up with Lee and soon met Kevin. Kevin was everything her upbringing trained her to want for a husband. He was intelligent and ambitious. They married and began a life together. Maria hoped marriage would fill the emptiness she felt inside. She had always wanted this: a husband, a home, and a family. But early in the marriage, Maria's sexual desire shut down. She lost attraction for her husband and all interest in sex. After the birth of their first child the situation grew worse. Feeling full of shame, she left her marriage. Her guilt and shame brought her into therapy. She was confused. Her values of a marriage, home, and family had crumbled around her. She explains, "I had to get out. I was dying inside."

Maria's story illustrates an addictive switch that is common for abuse survivors. Her sexual behaviors in high school and college had bulimic qualities—she entered relationships quickly and got out when they felt bad. Like a food bulimic who takes in large quantities of food and then vomits, Maria entered into a relationship too fast, then pushed it away when it felt toxic. Once married, however, the cycle changed and she became sexually anorexic. Her sexual feelings died. Maria could either be intensely sexual or completely shut down. There was no middle ground. Maria's upbringing left her internally scarred, impairing her ability to be intimate with anyone.

Heather

Heather's biological father died when she was a baby, so her first memories are only of her mother. As an adult, Heather's memories of her mother are bitter-sweet. They contain feelings of warmth mixed with sadness and loneliness. Undoubtedly, Heather picked up some of her mother's grief about the death of her husband. When Heather was four, her mother remarried a man named Joe, a surgeon from an elite social class. Joe became the light in her mother's life. Heather remembers everything changed when they went to live with Joe. She recalls long days, alone in her room, with no one to talk to or be with. In session, she describes these childhood memories using colors, "Everything was yellow until Joe came into our lives. Then everything turned gray."

Heather's mother and Joe were so wrapped up in their new marriage they failed to set limits for Heather. She frequently had no specific bedtime or mealtime. She was permitted to sit in front of the television for hours. Heather remembers falling asleep at the kitchen table once, and when Joe found her, he spanked her. Heather was terrified, humiliated, and confused. She doesn't remember where her mother was when this happened.

Heather had frequent stomach problems as a child, so her parents took her to see a doctor who was one of Joe's colleagues. This was in the 1970s before doctors might look into a nutritional issue or wonder about a child's anxiety levels. Instead, he recommended an enema. Heather remembers this humiliating experience: She was five years old, standing naked in the bathroom while Joe gave her the enema and waited until she used the bathroom. She felt ashamed and violated.

Heather remembers trying hard to please Joe and her mother by achieving good grades in school, and being a compliant, quiet child. She desperately wanted them to love her and include her.

Heather's mother worked on the weekends, and before she would leave, Heather remembers crawling into the warm spot in her bed and watching her dress for work. After her mother left, Heather remained in bed with Joe during the early morning hours. He would hold her. She loved these moments, but when she tried to wiggle loose, he held onto her and asked for just a few more minutes. She always stayed, grateful to be wanted, yet feeling awkward inside. Like Maria's relationship with her father, Heather's relationship with Joe contained a painful ambiguity. Moments of intense fear and humiliation merged with periodic times of affection.

At age eight, Heather's mother and Joe had a baby. Heather recalls the day her mother returned from the hospital with her new baby brother. She desperately wanted to stay home to be near her mother and see the baby, but Joe forced her to go to school. When she got there, she pretended to be sick so the nurse would send her home. Joe was so enraged that he sent Heather to her room for the rest of the day. She didn't get to see her mother or the baby and went to bed sad and alone. After this painful day, Heather felt like more of an outsider in her family.

Soon after her brother's birth, Heather accidentally discovered her stepfather's pornography collection in his closet. She learned to masturbate in the bathtub thinking of the images that she had seen in the magazines. Heather remembers spending what seemed like hours in the bathroom, finding comfort and pleasure from her orgasms. She felt immense relief because she could soothe her loneliness by herself. This was the beginning of a long relationship with sexuality that would eventually become an addiction.

In high school, Heather's academic performance exceeded her peers. She made outstanding grades and excelled in the German club. She was proud of her accomplishments because her parents liked to boast about them to their friends. But deep inside, she felt inadequate and alone. She never felt good enough.

During her freshman year she developed a crush on Mark. He was a star on the football team and liked by everyone. Even though he never dated Heather, he flirted with her. His attention fueled her adoration. She memorized everything about him–his license plate number, his class schedule, and she even changed from the Baptist church to the Catholic Church to be near him. At fourteen, Heather, like Maria, began showing signs of codependency. She was using a relationship to compensate for terrible feelings of isolation and pain.

When Heather was sixteen, Mark became sexually interested in her. Their relationship intensified, but Heather never felt like his girlfriend. Mark insisted they keep their relationship a secret, which left Heather feeling ashamed and rejected. She felt constantly challenged to do more, be more, try harder to earn Mark's love, just as she did with her mother and Joe. Heather's need to be perfect is a sign of her damaged sense of self-worth. Perfectionism is a symptom of codependency and love that is conditional. Heather never learned from her parents that she was worthy of love just because she was Heather. So, she accepted what little attention she could get from Mark because for her, the deprivation was familiar. She was repeating the deprivation of her childhood.

When Mark left for college, Heather's behavior changed. She began having sexual encounters with boys she didn't particularly like. When Mark came home during vacations, she dropped everything to have sex with him. When Heather graduated from high school, she moved out of state to be with him and enrolled in the same university. Like in high school, she and Mark continued their secret sexual relationship. Mark had a girlfriend so he only called Heather when he was drunk and wanted sex.

To hide her unmanageable feelings for Mark, Heather's sexual behavior escalated. Even though she was no longer under the watchful eye of her parents and their community, she was still concerned about being a good girl and protecting her reputation. So she tried to keep her sexual life separate from her college social life. She chose men she barely knew to have sex with. If a man wanted to become close to her, she dropped him.

In therapy, Heather relates her romantic life in brief spurts. "I only slept with guys I felt better than. I would meet one guy for breakfast, another for lunch, and another for dinner." Heather seduced men she met in restaurants, internships, libraries, or bars. She kept a list of how many men she slept with. The list included married men, friends' boyfriends, and brothers of previous boyfriends. These guys were always men she felt were "beneath" her. Heather explains,

I knew I was gaining a feeling of power with this behavior, but it came with so much pain because deep down I still yearned for Mark.

In therapy, years later, she wonders if the pain of her addiction to Mark created her sexually avoidant behavior.

I think deep down I told myself no one would ever have that kind of power over me again so I never let anyone get close.

What Heather is describing is the desperate attempt to heal her codependency with sexually addictive behavior. The pain of growing up in deprivation and isolation left her feeling unloved, inadequate, and ashamed. She felt like an outsider. She repeated this trauma with Mark. She felt that she never measured up. The constant yearning for his acceptance and love mirrored her yearning for parental connection. After repeated failures to get her needs met, Heather masked her codependency with sexual acting out. She gained a sense of control with seduction and flirtation, feeling new power with each man she had sex with. Her sexuality became a substitute for self-development, providing her with grandiose feelings that numbed her feelings of inferiority. Heather traded sexual power for authentic power.

Special note: Heather's list of sexual conquests is a common feature for girls and women who become addicted to sex. Keeping a list is one indicator of a growing sexual addiction.

Tori

Tori is the third child born to parents who thought they were finished having children. They already had a son, eight, and a daughter, seven. Tori's father was an anesthesiologist, her mother stayed home to raise the children. Their relationship was chaotic and intense. Tori's father was unable to be sexually faithful to her mother, and Tori's mother exhibited signs of being desperately addicted to her husband. Tori grew up in a household suffused with sexual energy and violence. She can't remember a time when sex was not on her mind and when she wasn't also feeling fear. From as early as she can remember, she knew her father was not faithful to her mother. Her earliest memory took place when she was five years old and she walked into her mother's room to find her swallowing pills. Her mother was crying. She yelled at Tori, "Get out of here." Tori remembers being frightened and confused. Later, Tori realized that this was her mother's first suicide attempt. Her mother had just learned of her husband's first affair. Tori also witnessed a great deal of violence by her older brother.

What I remember most about growing up is the physical violence between my brother and sister. My brother was mean, and from him I learned that men are violent. He was also using drugs. I just thought he was scary.

Tori recalls her brother being in and out of drug rehab. When he was gone the household would be temporarily tranquil. Tori's brother had a lot of power in the house.

When a teenage boy sets the tone for a home, he's taking the place of Dad. Since Tori's father was working or having affairs, he wasn't around. Tori's mother compensated for her loneliness and dependency by turning her energy onto her son. She turned to him for male companionship and guidance. This is an inappropriate role exchange which constitutes a form of emotional/sexual abuse.

When a son is prematurely put into the role of a man, his own developmental needs aren't met. As a result he acts out. Frequently, he uses drugs. He's angry with women because his mother's attention to him isn't appropriate. He learns that women are suffocating and impossible to please. Author and psychologist Ken Adams calls this form of mother/son enmeshment covert incest. In his book *Silently Seduced,* he outlines the devastating effects covert incest has for boys. In this environment, sibling incest is very common as the son acts out his rage erotically toward his sisters. Violence becomes part of the home and gets fused with sexual energy.

Tori learned to masturbate at an early age. She doesn't recall how or when she learned, but just that it was always her companion. "It was like breathing. I just always did it and didn't think anything of it." Tori's story is similar to Maria and Heather's in this way. All three learned as young girls how to self-soothe through masturbation.

In professional circles, when young girls are masturbating it can be a sign of early childhood sexual abuse. However, in each case, none of the women remember being sexually abused. Lack of memory does not rule out the possibility.

Many children are abused before the age of two, which can account for a lack of explicit memory. Furthermore, extreme fear compromises memory, as we will explore in greater detail in Chapter Six. We can assume that all three girls were under intense stress and fear. They were not attaching to their caregivers, who weren't safe or were physically and emotionally unavailable.

In Chapter Three we will explore the effects of fear and anxiety on the brain and neurological development, which accounts for the need a child may have for a soothing device. Without proper bonding and attachment, the girls found a way to comfort themselves and ease their heightened brain chemistry. Masturbation became the substitute for human connection.

Tori's sister left home at fifteen. Tori was only eight. She remembers being thrilled to have her mother all to herself. Her hope was to finally receive her mother's attention and care. It's interesting that Tori's brother was away in rehab and her sister found a way out of the house. These teenagers were profoundly lost and neglected. It's clear that Mom and Dad were too self-absorbed to be bothered with raising children, and yet here was Tori, still a little girl and left at home.

When Tori's siblings left, she remembers her mother becoming obsessed with her own business. Tori readied herself for school each morning, and came home in the afternoon to an empty house. She discovered new ways to soothe her loneliness. She began reading erotica and watching "real sex" on TV. "Thank God there was no Internet in our home at that time," she exclaims in therapy. As a woman in recovery, she now understands that her sexual and fantasy addiction would have been much more extreme with the avenues available to her online.

At fourteen, Tori's life began to spin out of control. Her mother discovered another one of her husband's affairs when she found a sex toy in his suitcase and a receipt with a young woman's name on it. Tori's mother flew into a rage and rallied her girls to accompany her to the woman's home. Tori remembers driving to the stranger's home with her mother and sister, but her mother refused to get out of the car, leaving Tori and her sister to confront the woman at the front door. The police were called and a confrontation led to a terrible fracture in the family. Tori's mom went to live with her older sister and Tori stayed with her dad. Tori's mother grossly abandoned her job as a mother by putting her daughters in the role of fighting her battles. It was reckless and damaging for both daughters. Tori remembers feeling afraid, angry, and humiliated during her mother's drama. This is emotional abuse and extreme neglect. Tori knew, deep down, she couldn't respect or trust her mother, so when her parents separated after this event, she stayed with her father. As always, Tori was left alone to raise herself.

Soon after this terrible incident, Tori lost her virginity to a boy at school. "The next day, he called me a whore to his friends," she recalls years later. Tori vowed she would never let a guy have power over her again. She broke up with the boy and pretended to not be hurt. To cover the pain of her loneliness at home, Tori's sexual behavior escalated. She began meeting boys, having sex with them, and not seeing them again. She didn't have sex with boys she knew from school, believing she could somehow salvage her reputation as a good girl. Now, as a woman, she wonders, "Who was I kidding? I talked about sex all the time. My girlfriends knew there was something different about me."

Tori always felt unique among her peers. She felt her interest in sex raised her to a higher, more sophisticated status. Yet underneath this feeling of superiority was a sad sense of shame. When Tori was fifteen, more chaos entered her family. Her sister and brother engaged in a court battle against one another. Her brother was accused of assaulting her sister. During this time, Tori's life was spinning out of control. Her weight plummeted from 112 to 87 pounds. Her mother lost her business and her parents declared bankruptcy.

This is a picture of unmanageability. Parents who cannot manage their financial lives, with two children in court and a daughter who was sexually acting out and becoming anorexic. Tori's sexual behavior was an attempt to hide the pain of her family situation. Her mother and father were addicted to each other, and acted out the drama of their marriage in front of their children. In an effort to escape the shame and anger of her situation, Tori began using sex in a reckless manner. When she was sixteen, Tori met a much older man at a nearby gym. There was instant attraction. The man took her to his house that same day. Tori describes the following scene:

He penetrated me anally and it hurt so bad. He bit me during oral sex, and it was so painful that my legs were shaking. I was scared … I had never done this before. I just froze and left my body. I remember there was a woman in his house when I got there, but she left. She must have known what was going to happen. When I got home, I remember putting a temporary tattoo on my neck to hide his teeth marks. I remember feeling really dirty. I never went back to that gym. I thought it was my fault. It took me a long time to realize it was rape.

As Tori tells her story, it comes out in pieces, almost like she's choking. The trauma of the rape still echoes in her voice. Her body still carries fear and shame. After this horrifying experience, her behavior intensified.

My life became more sexualized in college. I was constantly flirting, and working out and trying to look the best I could. No one's boyfriend was safe around me. I slept with whomever I wanted to. I remember my mom telling me that since I wasn't blond and blue-eyed, I'd never be beautiful, and I think I spent all my time trying to compensate for that. Everything in my world was about sex. The music I listened to and the clothes I put on. I lived to make men want me. I wanted to be the girl a guy was thinking about when he had sex with his girlfriend. I wanted to be his fantasy. If my father hadn't been sending me plenty of money each week, I would have been a stripper or an escort.

Tori learned from listening to guys talk that there was a right way and wrong way to please a guy sexually, and she wanted to know the right way. When Tori met Todd, who was thirty years old and divorced, he was the first man she ever pleased orally. After he had an orgasm he told her, "No woman has ever been able to make me orgasm like that!" and Tori felt wonderful. She felt powerful. In her mind, oral sex gave her complete power. After about a year, Tori began having sex with other men to boost her sense of power. The relationship with Todd lasted three years, and Tori's need for sex grew stronger as her feelings of insecurity grew.

Then Tori met Chad. She broke up with Todd one weekend and started dating Chad the next. Chad was Tori's age, educated, and making plans to join the Navy. Tori wanted to be faithful to Chad. She wanted this relationship to be different from her others. She remembers that Chad masturbated every day, watched porn, and had a sister who was a porn star. Their father had purchased a breast augmentation for his daughter when she entered the sex industry. None of these issues were red flags for Tori. She thought she was in love.

Like many sex and love addicts, Tori found a partner who came from a family similar to her own. She and Chad both came from backgrounds where sex infused the family environment. Tori recalls that in the first ten days she knew Chad, they had sex seventeen times. She thought that he must really love her to want her so much. She felt so powerful. She was only twenty-two. Like many sex addicts, Tori also had a problem with alcohol. As her attachment to Chad intensified, her drinking escalated. She was trying to be faithful to him, but found herself feeling weak with feelings of love and dependency. She was terrified of becoming her mother. When Chad suddenly broke up with her, Tori was stunned and began to crumble. Something in her gave up on the idea of love and she decided to go back to using men for sex.

Barbara

Barbara came from an upper middle-class family. Her father was a doctor, her mother a homemaker. Before the age of four, Barbara remembers happy times with her father. She remembers him as warm and kind. "He held me and smiled at me." Barbara doesn't have pleasant memories of her mother. She remembers her mother as unaffectionate and unloving, always ironing, gardening, or cleaning. She also remembers her mother having a vodka martini each night before dinner. Her mother threw lavish parties to entertain her husband's colleagues, and Barbara remembers helping out with these events to earn her mother's approval. But it never seemed to work. Barbara felt disconnected from her mother, which intensified her yearning for her father's attention.

When Barbara was four, there was a family incident that left her feeling afraid and confused. In Barbara's words, she recalls,

... standing at the top of the stairwell, and they were taking my dad away on a stretcher. They were taking him away and I didn't know why, and I didn't know if I'd ever see him again.

Barbara has no memory of the rest of that day. Apparently, she was left alone to make sense of this terrible event. Where was her mother? Why didn't she help Barbara make sense of what was happening? Was her father physically ill or did he suffer some type of emotional breakdown? The answers to these questions are still not clear for Barbara even today. When her father was taken from their home, Barbara experienced unnecessary fear and disorientation due to the lack of adult reassurance. Barbara believed her father might be dying. When a child is left alone to make sense of something frightening or tragic, her brain can't metabolize the events in a way to feel safe. Barbara felt profoundly frightened and abandoned that day. As an adult, she still has trouble processing the memory of the event and cannot recall what the rest of her family did to cope, or what exactly happened to her father. For these reasons, an event that could have been painful, but not traumatic, became tragic. In Chapter Six, we will explore what happens to the memory during trauma and why Barbara still has trouble piecing together the events of that day.

After her father's trouble, Barbara remembers her family as cold and distant. Her parents weren't affectionate toward each other. They seemed to be emotionally shut down. Her father had unpredictable moods. On a good day, he could play with Barbara in the backyard or read her a bedtime story. But on a bad day, he had an explosive temper and became physically abusive. Since Barbara had bonded with her father early in her life, she was shocked by his new behavior and totally unprepared. Her father was her refuge. Now he seemed lost to her. She couldn't make sense of his abusive treatment, so she internalized that something must be wrong with her.

Barbara spent her energy trying to regain her father's warm attention. She excelled in school to please him. She tried to adapt to his moods, spending hours with him watching baseball on TV. When he raged, she tried to soothe him. She studied him and tried to be like him. But eventually she became weary. To soothe herself she turned to food. She craved ice cream, candy bars, and chocolate. The sugar helped her hide the emptiness she felt inside.

When a child works hard to earn a parents love and approval, she has no time to develop her own interests or desires. She lives to please someone else. Personality development is stunted, and the results are painful. In Chapter Three, we'll examine in more detail what happens to children when their development is damaged in this way.

As Barbara became a teenager, her attempts to connect with her father changed. She began provoking his anger, preferring the intensity of an argument to his painful dismissal. Their fighting resembled an unhappy married couple more than a father-daughter relationship. Since Barbara's parents had very little connection, the primary intensity in the home was between Barbara and her dad.

Barbara began gaining weight, which greatly displeased her father. He told her she looked "fat" and tried to monitor her eating. Barbara began to hide her food. She ate late at night, alone, in her room. Her eating became an expression of rage. The anger she felt toward her father was turned onto herself.

Barbara was a very isolated teenager. Her primary relationships were with her father and with food. The relationship with her father became more strained when she was sixteen and her cousin Ed visited while on military leave. He asked Barbara to meet him downtown for a beer. When Barbara's father found out she had joined her cousin at a bar, he was furious and lost control. He hit Barbara so hard that he broke her eardrum. The next day Barbara's mother took her to the doctor because her ear was bleeding. She never once offered Barbara any emotional support.

Deep inside, Barbara felt vindicated when she told the doctor how her injury had occurred. Since the doctor was a colleague of her father's, Barbara felt a sense of power sharing how her father had hit her, knowing he would have to face his colleague.

Even though Barbara's father eventually apologized, it was meaningless to her. She just felt cold. Barbara had adapted to her father's abusive behavior by shutting down. She was cold and distant from her family. In fact, she was aloof from everyone. She had no close relationships with boys or girls her age. Barbara was living in a kind of social deprivation. In Chapter Six, we will examine sexual and emotional anorexia. Barbara's story illustrates how this form of psychological isolation can interact with compulsive overeating. Barbara used food to replace the human relationships she had learned to distrust and avoid.

In college, Barbara replaced the intensity with her father with her first romance. She met Adam in a bar one night. Adam was twenty-eight, divorced and out of work, but Barbara felt flattered by his attention. In no time Barbara and Adam were spending lots of time together. Adam was struggling to get back into school, and Barbara found that helping him with his homework gratified her. She felt powerful and needed. She knew Adam admired her, which gave her a sense of control. Barbara lost her virginity in this relationship. However, she never felt like she loved him. Part of her stayed separate from Adam, so when he ended the relationship after a year, she was sad, but oddly detached. It's as if she never really bonded to Adam. Part of her still remained frozen and numb.

Barbara learned to be cold growing up in her family. Furthermore, the intense relationship with her father filled important space in her heart and soul. On an unconscious level, she had no room for another love. Her father was her primary relationship. The psychological bond between them kept Barbara hostage and unavailable for age-appropriate relationships. In Chapter Three, we will discuss how this kind of father-daughter bond is a form of emotional abuse.

In graduate school, Barbara met Jerome at the hospital where she was completing an internship. Jerome was a surgery technician, but also a drug addict with little ambition. He lived at home with his mother and spent most of his free time with the guys from his neighborhood, finding various ways to acquire drugs and money. Barbara found him wildly attractive. Shortly after they began dating, Jerome moved in with Barbara. She tried everything to keep Jerome happy. She allowed him to borrow her car and gave him money. She recalls feeling desperate for his love and attention.

At one point, he lost a bet in a poker game and asked her to have sex with one of his friends to pay the bet. She agreed. Barbara wanted his love so badly she compromised her dignity to protect the illusion that Jerome loved her. But the relationship remained tumultuous. Barbara remembers terrible fighting as she pleaded with Jerome to spend more time with her. Her efforts failed to give her what she needed, so her behavior switched. She began having one-night stands with other men to deal with her painful loneliness. In later chapters, we will follow the progression of Barbara's addiction to men and sex.

Like Maria and Heather, Barbara's sexual behavior escalated with her attempt to cope with codependency. Her unmet childhood needs were running her adult choices. Her desperate search for love and underlying insecurity put her in humiliating situations. Sex with other men became her painkiller. It became her drug. In this way, we can understand the intimate mix of codependency and sexual addiction. The sex addiction is an attempt to stop the pain of codependency.

Painful Connections

Reading Maria, Heather, Tori, and Barbara's story may leave you with unpleasant feelings. It's difficult to witness another's abuse or compulsive behavior. With an open mind, you might see the trauma that led each woman into her painful addictive habits. In each woman's story, there are similar themes: households with no boundaries around sex and violence. Mother's who weren't available to their daughters. For each woman there were early experiences with secretive sexuality that created fear or rejection. And the fathers in each story couldn't manage their own sexuality in mature, healthy ways. These four women were born into families that set them up for an addiction to sex and love. However, there are many other factors that contribute to the development of this addiction that will be addressed in the next two chapters.

Am I addicted to love or sex?

When does a relationship cross the line from intense to addictive? Since all relationships feel intoxicating at the beginning how do we know when a relationship is in trouble? If you suspect after reading this chapter that you might be a sex and love addict, these questions will help you think about your romantic patterns. The questions come from a number of sources, including the fellowship of Sex and Love Addicts Anonymous. The questions are not meant to be a full diagnostic tool. Deciding that you're a sex and love addict is a very personal decision. Only you can make that decision. However, if you find yourself answering yes to more than three of these questions, carefully review the criteria for addiction that follows.

* Do you change relationships often, sure the next one will be "right"?
* Have you tried to control your relationship patterns with little success?
* Do you feel shame or fear as a result from your sexual activities?
* Do you feel empty when you are alone?
* Do you use substances such as food, work, drugs, or alcohol to avoid feelings?
* Have you neglected responsibilities, such as family, friends, hobbies, work, or yourself due to time spent or preoccupied with romantic partners?
* Do you spend large amounts of time grooming to be seductive, flirting, or seeking romantic partners? Do you wear provocative clothing in an effort to attract?
* Have you been sexual or romantic with inappropriate people: a boss, a married person, your doctor, a person who comes to you for help, or a person in a subordinate position to you?
* Have you experienced periods of inactivity from sexual pursuits during which you were excessive or anorexic in other areas of your life, such as eating or spending?
* Are you spending large amounts of time online in chat rooms, dating sites, or viewing sexually explicit material?
* Do you assign magical qualities to others, idealize them and pursue them, and blame them for not fulfilling your fantasies and expectations?
* Do you become sexually or emotionally involved with people without knowing them?
* Have you been a victim of overt or covert incest as a child or teen? (We will explain this more in future chapters.)
* Do you have difficulty saying "no" to sexual or romantic partners?
* Do you act outside your value system with sexual and romantic partners?

Criteria for sex and love addiction

Addiction experts have identified the following criteria that indicate an addiction. If you answered "yes" to three or more of the questions above, it doesn't mean you have an addiction. However, if you respond "yes" to the following criteria, your romantic life has likely become addictive.

- loss of time with family members, hobbies, and friends
- an experience of being "high" followed by secrecy and shame
- negative consequences (which may include health problems and financial problems)
- obsessive preoccupation with the relationship or sex
- attempts to stop your behavior (or obsession) fail and bring considerable irritability and distress
- your behavior becomes riskier or more intense

If you have an addiction you will identify with most of the criteria. Your addiction is taking more of your time and effort to maintain. Your use of sex and romance feels necessary for life to hold meaning. If sex or love has become your drug of choice you're in a painful paradox. You have a valid need for a relationship that has been twisted into an addiction. Sex and love addiction is a disease of loneliness. It is a disease fueled by shame and despair. By naming the disease, healing can begin.

Sex and love addiction is a complex compulsion to use romance, people, and sexuality to feel alive. It is a difficult reality to face. But others before you have faced it, and have found a new freedom from the process of healing. In the chapters to come, you will learn more about this disease and about how to heal. It can be very disturbing to read about these women, their stories, and the reasons for this disease. You might want to put the book down–or throw it against the wall.

This is normal. Take it gently and keep in mind that facing sexual issues brings up shame. It takes great courage and integrity to face your sexuality. Unlike other addictions, sex and love addiction is core to the self. Healing this disease may possibly be the most difficult yet most rewarding work you do in your lifetime. When you address sexuality, you face your spirit.

Chapter Two
A Dis-ease of Cultural Inheritance

*Our culture gives girls the message that their bodies, their
lives, and their femaleness demand an apology.*
Dr. Christiane Northrup, *Women's Bodies, Women's Wisdom*[1]

If reading Chapter One has left you feeling uncomfortable, frightened, or angry, that's understandable. This is difficult material. And you're one of the brave women taking a risk to look at your relational behavior. As you embark on this journey of sexual recovery, you'll find there isn't much cultural awareness or support for your process. You may be feeling very much alone as you explore this book and what it means for you. You may be wondering, *How could I possibly be a sex and love addict?*

The answer to this question isn't simple. It requires exploring both your culture and family of origin. In this chapter, we'll examine our society and the four cultural beliefs women inherit. Cultural influences for women often are minimized or overlooked when a woman is facing an addiction. Addiction, however, is a powerful coping strategy for living in a culture that does not give women the same status as men. Addiction is a method of compensating for powerlessness. When women are put in an inferior position to men, they find ways to regain power, overtly or covertly. Understanding cultural dynamics sheds light on power dynamics that eventually lead to addictive behavior and pain.

Women inherit four particularly damaging cultural beliefs. These beliefs create incredible shame because they present a sexual double for women. The double bind is a setup for sex and love addiction.

Four Cultural Beliefs

Northrup explains how

... healing cannot occur for women until they have critically examined and changed some of the beliefs and assumptions that we all unconsciously inherit and internalize from our culture.[2]

The key issue for healing destructive romantic patterns, then, is to identify unhealthy beliefs that create shame and change them. Remember, shame fuels addiction. Negative beliefs create shame and drive the need for escape. Addictive behavior provides a necessary escape from unbearable thoughts and beliefs. The interaction between negative beliefs and addictive acting out becomes a powerful cycle that is repetitive and enduring.

Dr. Patrick Carnes, a leading researcher and author in the field of sexual addiction, illustrates the relationship between a person's negative belief system and addiction. He has designed the cycle of addiction that begins with a belief, grows into impaired thinking, and results in preoccupation and compulsive behavior.[3]

The Addictive System

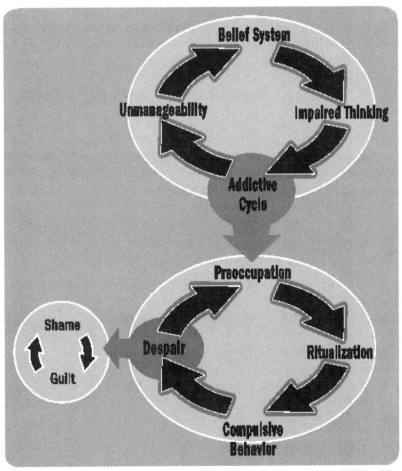

©2094 The Addictive System, Dr. Patrick Carnes, Ph.D.

Notice from Carnes' diagram that when the belief system gets triggered, addictive behavior soon follows. Without intervention, the cycle moves from belief to despair.

Harmful Beliefs

For individuals addicted to sex or relationships, Carnes has illustrated four core beliefs that fuel the addiction. They are:

- I am a bad, unworthy person.
- No one would love me as I am.
- If I have to rely on others to meet my needs, they will not be met.
- Sex is my most important need; or my most important sign of love; or my most terrifying need.[4]

Perhaps you can relate to Carnes' belief system. You may feel that no one could possibly love you if they really knew you. It's difficult for you to trust people, especially romantic partners. You may feel that if someone is sexual with you, it means they love you. You may have developed a fear of sex and relationships. These beliefs result in a profound sense of shame. They also contribute to a deep loneliness.

In addition to the four beliefs outlined by Carnes, you may have inherited one or even all four of the cultural beliefs that exist for women. These cultural beliefs drive painful romantic and sexual behavior. They are designed to teach you how to be "feminine." Femininity is a sociological construction, separate from biology. Biologically, you are a woman. Culturally, you are taught how to be feminine. You are taught by messages in our literature, advertising, and film. Ideas of how to be feminine are supported by our government, churches, and schools. They are in our myths, legends, and folk tales. These ideas about women, sex, and love are so institutionalized they seem real. They are:

- I must be "good" in order to be worthy of love.
- If I am sexual, I am "bad."
- I am not really a woman unless someone desires me sexually and/or romantically.
- I must be sexual to be lovable.

In the following pages, you will find a brief discussion of each belief. Chapter Five will provide illustrations of some of the ways women act out each belief in their romantic lives.

Cultural Belief Number One

I must be good to be worthy of love.
In *Reviving Ophelia,* author and psychologist Mary Pipher, Ph.D, explains how adolescent girls "are expected to sacrifice...parts of themselves...on the altar of

social acceptability and to shrink their souls down to a petite size."[5] She calls this the "indoctrination into the code of goodness," which is largely unchanged since the 1950s. How often do we hear "be a good girl" or "if you are good, then you can have…"

The code of goodness is like basic training for girls. It requires girls to behave in certain ways that make people comfortable. Girls should be nice, non-threatening, and willing to serve. In her book, Pipher calls America a "girl-destroying" place, and she illustrates how girls are encouraged to ignore their knowledge, hopes, and power in order to someday find an identity through a partner. If her partner has status, she will, too. If her partner has power, she will, too. Although the gender handicap for girls is changing, girls are still receiving negative messages. Although many parents work to teach their daughters strength of character and offer them choices, our culture undermines their best efforts to raise healthy daughters.

Some girls successfully conform to the standard of goodness and appear happy, well-balanced, and "normal." A young adolescent may not identify the sacrifices she makes in order to be a good girl. Femininity training (the pressure to be nice and please others) creates pressure for girls and some withdraw emotionally as they make efforts to conform. They may become quiet, shy, and isolated. Parents may wonder what is happening as they watch their daughter retreat during the middle school years.

Some adolescents become angry. In an effort to conform to the good-girl standard, they turn the anger inside instead of expressing it outwardly. Anger turned inside can result in depression. She may appear tired and confused, listless or bored, showing little interest in her regular activities. Anger turned inward can also result in an eating disorder. Food is a successful way to stuff or numb feelings of anger. While some girls struggle to hide their anger, others are more overt and may appear rebellious, hostile, and loud. They may start drinking alcohol or using drugs to numb their feelings.

Some girls begin sexually acting out at this age. Sexuality becomes a way for girls to go around the code of goodness and still attract a boy, feel powerful, or get attention. In this manner, sex becomes an angry response to a cultural code that is suffocating and unfair. Femininity training distorts sexual development and, sadly, a young woman may not see her body as something special that is hers to cherish.

As girls become women, the struggle to be good doesn't disappear. Northrup agrees with Pipher, saying our society demands "that women…ignore or turn away from their hopes and dreams…"[6] Northrup explains that when women deny "their needs for self-expression and self-actualization [it] causes enormous emotional pain." Conforming to cultural standards of femininity means that as a woman, you must relinquish your power and, therefore, yourself. In doing so, you earn the right to be loved.

Cultural Belief Number Two

If I am sexual, I am bad.

Sexual feelings and desires are a natural part of being alive. Sexual energy is creative energy. But for many women, sex is something to be mistrusted and hidden. Religion plays a significant role in complicating sexuality for women. In many religious traditions, sexual purity has higher value than having sexual needs or desires. Most women are taught that sex is somehow dangerous or bad, but should be saved for the sanctity of marriage when it will suddenly be an expression of love.

Maria explained in therapy how she couldn't flip the switch that would allow her to be sexual with her husband.

Sex had always been considered a sin...and I spent years trying to hide from myself and others my sexual feelings. So, when I met a man that seemed like a wonderful person and decided to marry him, I couldn't sustain sexual interest in him...he was good, I was good, sex was bad. In my body, I couldn't reconcile this problem. If we were sexual together, I felt we were somehow bad and I know he felt it.

In many Christian churches, men are warned against the temptations of women, as if by association they will be brought into sexual sin. Church teachings unite with cultural forces that perpetuate the belief that sex is dirty. Implicit in this belief is the split between Madonna and whore; the Madonna is the virginal symbol of sexual purity that women should emulate as good mothers and wives. The whore, on the other hand, is the woman who breaks the rules, ruins marriages, and demonstrates her sexuality.

Author Charlotte Kasl highlights how "women have been taught to disconnect from sexual feelings, to hate, only secretly enjoy, or feel ashamed of them."[7] We can find examples of Kasl's statement in American entertainment. For instance, consider the '60's television show *Bewitched*. Samantha gives up her witchcraft to please her husband Darren, who is uncomfortable with the truth that Samantha is a witch. His mortal mind cannot make room for her magic. The idea is that magic, or witchcraft, is bad. It can't be trusted. Samantha's efforts to please her husband and become a "normal" wife are designed to entertain the audience. She learns to cook, clean, and manage a household without the use of her magic.

Her magic, however, is part of her. It's her core. Occasionally, she finds herself in situations where she must use magic. When Darren discovers Samantha has used her magic, he gets angry, yells at her, and pouts until she makes efforts to apologize and soothe his wounded ego. The show takes an interesting twist at times.

Occasionally, Darren needs Samantha's magic. In these moments, the two seem bonded and happy as they join together to do something bad. They take pleasure in her magic and, somehow, the fact that magic is their secret increases the enjoyment. *Bewitched* is supposed to be a lighthearted comedy. But in fact, it contains a kind of darkness.

Samantha's marriage to Darren puts her in a double bind. Samantha gives up her magic for love. She sacrifices an essential part of herself in order to be with Darren. When we decide to marry, we all make sacrifices. This could include moving to a new town, giving up time with friends or a hobby, or even something simpler, like sharing the TV remote. Love requires us to periodically honor the wishes of our partner over our own. However, if we sacrifice a core part of ourselves for love, the sacrifice becomes self-abuse.

Samantha's magic is core to who she is. By conforming to Darren's belief that magic is bad, Samantha essentially colludes in believing that she is defective. She takes on a negative belief about herself. Samantha's attempts to avoid using magic are painful to watch. At times, she must clench her teeth in an effort to contain her natural urge to use magic.

Let's think of Samantha's magic as a metaphor for sexuality. The irony becomes that in order for her to be "worthy" of her husband's love, her sexuality must exist on his terms. In other words, unless Darren needs sex, Samantha's sexuality shouldn't exist. If she uses her sexuality for her own reasons, she risks his rejection, disapproval, and anger. The message is that her sexuality is bad. It can't be trusted, controlled, or contained. She can only be sexual when Darren gives her permission. When the two share Samantha's gift of sexuality, they enjoy each other, but they have a secret. Sex, like Samantha's magical powers, stays hidden.

The obvious question is why would Samantha make this kind of sacrifice for love? In a culture that raises girls and women as second-class citizens, giving up everything for love is part of the fantasy implicit in fairy tales, romance novels, movies, and television. Giving up the self for love is not a huge price when the alternative is being alone.

Cultural Belief Number Three

I am not really a woman unless someone desires me sexually or romantically.
For many women, there is a belief that "beauty is my most important source of power." In our culture, beauty is power. We love beautiful people. Our fascination with Hollywood speaks to the love of beauty. Beauty is aligned with sexual desirability. Sexual desirability is aligned with femininity. Therefore, Cultural Belief Number Three is about power, desire, and beauty. Think about when these ideas first come together for young girls. Consider Disney's *Sleeping Beauty, Cinderella* or *The Little Mermaid*. These fairy tales take root in the minds and hearts of many young girls and women.

When asked to remember favorite stories, women can describe in detail their love for fairy tales. As young girls, fairy tales provide women with role models. Their pictures, songs, and clothing are everywhere. At Halloween, young girls dress in costumes complete with imitation glass slippers, flowing long gowns, and dazzling faux jewelry.

Many women carry these fairy tales deep in their psyche. The story of *Cinderella* is the archetypical fairy tale. Cinderella is rescued from a life of poverty and abuse by her prince. She endures horrible conditions while living with her wicked stepmother and stepsisters, until one night she's transformed into a beautiful maiden by her fairy godmother. It's then that she's finally recognized and pursued by Prince Charming. Her pain is erased when she's chosen to be his wife. And, of course, the tale ends "happily ever after." It's as if her real life has just begun. She's finally her "true" self. For many women, this myth holds power. Until they meet a Prince, they put life on hold.

In *Sex and the City,* season two devotes an entire episode to fairy tales. The main character, Carrie Bradshaw, talks about women's desire to be princesses. At the end of the episode, Carrie is desperately running to meet the midnight ferry and leaves behind one tiny little shoe, which is retrieved by her date and helps him find her. The similarity to Cinderella's glass slipper is no mistake. *Sex and the City* is essentially a modern-day fairy tale. One married woman explains "I love the show because I momentarily escape into the fantasy world of high fashion, life without my kids, and the thrill of a first date."

Sex and the City creates a fantasy that revolves around the search for Prince Charming. Carrie and her friends make the constant search for love appear glamorous. Although it has an obsessive tone, the show's focus on romance suggests it's normal to wander through life, waiting to be "found" by a Prince.

Disney's *The Little Mermaid* is a fascinating example of the sacrifices women make for love. Ariel gives up her voice so she can become human and pursue the man she's fallen in love with, a man she's never even met. The power of her love is so intense that she contracts with the wicked Ursula to win her prince's heart, and in doing so, risks her own life. The sacrifice Ariel makes for love is no surprise for many women. In their own addictive pursuit of love and romance, they make similar choices. Women sacrifice their power by silencing their own voices. They lose their ability to articulate needs and desires. In order to have love, women sacrifice authentic self-expression. Consider Jane's words:

I never felt beautiful, so I always needed to find a way to make a man notice me. Sometimes I could do this by the way I dressed or by being flirtatious. Sometimes, I used intelligence. When I got a man's attention, I felt better…more powerful. More like me. The intensity of a man's attention was intoxicating. Without it, I didn't know myself and I couldn't function very well. From the attention I gained energy and strength. I felt like a woman because I was wanted. But I never felt safe. I could never trust. I didn't realize the reason I couldn't trust him was because I couldn't trust me. I wasn't sure how far I would go to earn a man's attention. I never knew how much of me I would sacrifice for him.

Cultural Belief Number Four:
I must be sexual to be lovable.
Kasl documents how there are few models of healthy sexuality for women in our

culture. "Seductive or pornographic images of women abound on television, in advertising, in family-oriented catalogues–in short, everywhere."[8] Kasl argues that we have a "long-standing conditioning in our culture that says sex is love…"

In Hollywood, love is portrayed as two adults having sex. Sex happens fast in the movies. Sexual intensity is marketed as sexual intimacy. Many of us learn how to be sexual and romantic from TV and movies. Sex as love becomes fused in our minds.

For example, in *Sex and the City,* sex is an indicator of love. In one episode, Carrie is convinced that her new boyfriend must not like her very much because after the third date, he still hasn't tried to sleep with her. She gets panicky, so she dresses provocatively for their fourth date. When her attempts to seduce Aiden fail, she finally confronts him. He tells her he's waiting until he feels the relationship reaches a certain depth before he desires a sexual relationship with her. This shocks Carrie and her friends. *Sex and the City* gives female audiences entertaining images of liberated, single women–a huge leap forward from the days of *Bewitched*–but it also promotes a damaging belief that being sexual is the same as being lovable.

For mothers of daughters, this particular cultural belief is a painful one. If a mother wants to raise her daughter to cherish her sexuality as a sacred expression of her commitment to a relationship, she encounters little cultural support. One mother describes her ambivalence about a bulletin board in her daughter's bedroom.

There are pictures of beautiful women cut out from magazines all over her wall. These women are erotically posed with few clothes on. My daughter studies these women. She mimics these women. While I want her to have role models, this is not exactly what I had in mind. I don't want to shame her by removing them, but how do I compensate with images of women that are powerful but not sexual?

This mother's concern is real. Where can she find images as compelling as what her daughter sees in media and advertising to teach her how to be a woman?

The Four Cultural Beliefs: A Double Bind
Consider the four cultural beliefs for women in light of the following definition of double bind. The American Heritage Dictionary calls a double bind:

A psychological impasse created when contradictory demands are made of an individual so that no matter which directive is followed, the response will be construed as incorrect…a punishing and inescapable dilemma.[9]

The four cultural beliefs set up a double bind. To be worthy of love, you must be "good." But if you are sexual, you are "bad." Yet you must be desired to be a woman. So how can you be a sexual woman and still be a good person? It's a double bind. It's a crazy-making "punishing and inescapable dilemma." You cannot be both Madonna and whore. When it comes to relationships and sexuality, you are at an impasse, "a road or passage having no exit…a difficult situation offering no workable escape."[10]

Sex and love addiction provides an "escape" to the double bind. The addiction serves as an outlet for this impossible cultural inheritance. As a sex and love addict, you attempt to avoid the "punishing and inescapable" cultural dilemma that you are unworthy of love. Understood in this way, sex and love addiction is a brilliant survival mechanism. The disease gives you the illusion of being desired, being worthy and having love.

Double Bind/Double Shame

To cope with a double bind, you may be living a double life. Parts of your life are secret and hidden. The stories in Chapter One illustrate how a sexual double life begins. Heather, Maria, Tori, and Barbara each found ways to be sexual and, at the same time, conform to the standards of "goodness" set up for women. They each had the self they showed the world, and the self they tried to hide. In each story, the women experience feelings of shame, a sense of being dirty, and a terrible loneliness that comes from hiding the self. Each woman thought she alone had a problem.

Some of you have done considerable work to heal the cultural messages you inherit, and exposed them for the lies that they are. As a result, you may have enjoyed certain sexual freedoms. However, if your romantic and sexual patterns have become chronically destructive, you face another layer of shame: the shame that is a direct consequence of compulsively using relationships to feel OK. If you are struggling with addictive relationships, your behavior consistently violates your inner truth and values. As a result, when you begin to heal from this addiction and realize the pain you have caused yourself and others, you may feel very small and alone.

Keep in mind that you did not create this *dis-ease* by yourself. It has been a way for you to handle the shame of being a woman living with impossible cultural standards for femininity. Sex and love addiction is a desperate attempt to live within narrow, damaging sexual margins. It's not about morality. It's a disease of cultural inheritance.

Chapter Three
A Dis-ease of Psychological Isolation

*Clinical experience informs us that one of the most,
if not the most, terrifying human experiences is
psychological isolation.*
Dr. Christiane Northrup, *Women's Bodies, Women's Wisdom*[1]

Attachment theory teaches us that, without relationships, the human brain does not develop appropriately. Biologically, a child is born to grow and mature in relationships with other people. She's designed for connection. Traditionally, women have been shamed for their focus on relationships. They've been labeled weak, needy or dependent in their efforts to make connections with loved ones.

Dr. Jean Baker Miller rejects the notion that a yearning for connection is a weakness or a sign of instability. She argues that in order for an individual to develop a sense of self, there must be a relationship in which to do this.[2] Relationships foster human growth, individual development, and psychological health.

Dr. Judith Jordan explains that "self-development" is in fact "relational development."[3] The delicate concept of self forms within relationships, not separate from them. Miller and Jordan place human connection as the fundamental location of psychological development. This assertion challenges us to reexamine the importance of human connection, and reject the notion that the need for connection is a sign of weakness.[4]

In order to appreciate the complicated nature of love and sex addiction for women, it's imperative to first recognize the terror of psychological isolation. Psychological isolation is more than being alone. It is the feeling of being "locked out" of human connection. It is the belief you're shut out of a relationship because there's something wrong with you. The word loneliness doesn't quite capture the shame of psychological isolation. Shame creates the belief that you are to blame for being lonely. Something about you is broken or defective. *No matter what you try, you always feel wrong.*

Isolation and Trauma

Psychological isolation is traumatic. If a child cannot depend on her caregivers for physical comfort or emotional support, bonding and attachment needs are damaged. For a child, psychological isolation produces fear. Chronic fear causes significant problems for a child's brain chemistry and self-development. In his book *The Developing Mind,* Dr. Daniel Siegal explains how

... for the infant and young child, attachment relationships are the major environmental factors that shape the development of the brain...human connections create neuronal connections.[5]

Children need human connection in order to properly develop. Healthy human relationships grow the brain. In *Keep Your Brain Alive - 83 Neurobic Exercises,* Dr Lawrence Katz and Manning Rubin asserts the following.

If I showed you a picture of what your brain was doing when you were involved with another person, you wouldn't believe it. There are specialized areas that are just devoted to this. And the absence of human interaction is just deadly for the brain.[6]

In isolation, a child will not fully develop proper neuronal connections necessary for human bonding and attachment. Therefore, psychological isolation is a form of emotional abuse. Siegal and Lawrence support what Miller found in the '70's–human connection and healthy relationships are absolutely necessary for human growth. In other words, healthy relationships are necessary for healthy self-development. Women who struggle with issues of sex and love addiction rarely experienced healthy connection with caregivers in their formative years. Their stories are full of relationship pain. Maria, Barbara, Heather, and Tori each experienced fractured relationships with their caregivers. Healthy bonding and attachment didn't happen in their families. They learned to bond with people who were abusive and self-centered. Relationships were not safe places to be.

So how could someone with relationship pain in her past find herself addicted to love, sex, and relationships? Isn't that a contradiction? On the surface, yes. It's an interesting paradox. But think about what happens when you fall in love. The early intense feelings that the body generates in the initial stages of romance leave you feeling energized and excited. You feel great. The chemistry of early love is intoxicating. Since a traumatized brain has a lack of proper chemistry, the body attaches to powerful love chemicals and finally feels normal. You might invest all of yourself at once in the early stages of a relationship. You may become deeply and immediately involved with someone without really knowing him or her. This is fertile ground for love to become addiction.

Neurochemical Results of Chronic Psychological Isolation

Seigal calls caregivers the "architects of...brain development."[7] Children learn from their caregivers how to love. If a child is born into a family who deeply desires her and creates time to nurture her, she will likely find that her adult relationships are satisfying and sustaining. Her brain will maintain the necessary neurochemistry for happy relationships. Serotonin and dopamine, hormones the brain produces for attachment and feelings of well-being, will not be compromised. She is born wired and ready for love and attachment–and her environment allows her brain to develop naturally and do its work.

However, in families where abuse is the norm, children are at risk for chemical disruptions in the brain. Psychological isolation alters the brain. When a child is frightened, her brain prepares the body for pain. A powerful neurochemical process begins. Her amygdyla, the fight or flight receptor in the brain, is activated. The stress hormones adrenaline, norepinephrine, and cortisol are released into the child's system, preparing her for fight/flight. These chemicals are powerful, designed for action and protection. They are not designed for bonding. Over time, the chronic release of stress hormones damage the neural networks necessary for the transmission of dopamine and serotonin. Chronic fear damages the brain's ability to feel good.

When abuse happens repeatedly in a family, children turn away from connection. They learn it is not safe. Gradually, a young brain will adapt to isolation and stress. In other words, her brain, originally wired for connection, will adapt to trauma. When fear is chronic, her brain becomes attached to chemicals that are not for building relationships, but for running from them. The brain, designed at birth for love and connection, is now what Carnes calls a "hijacked brain."[8]

In *The Neuroscience of Psychotherapy*, Louis Cozolino, Ph.D, explains that due to the importance of safety and bonding in the early construction of the brain,

... the most devastating types of trauma are those that occur at the hands of caretakers. Physical and sexual abuse by parents not only traumatizes children, but also deprives them of the healing interactions.[9]

Research supports that "healing interactions" have the ability to lessen the long-term impact of trauma. Children who receive comfort from an adult during stress have less PTSD symptoms. For children who experience abuse from their caregivers, however, healthy support from an adult is often absent. There is no place to turn. The resulting isolation actually compounds the trauma, adding additional stress to her brain.

Maria

Maria recalls a time when she was four or five years old. She remembers being lonely and afraid in bed one night and calling her mother's name. Instead, her father came into her room. Feeling fear, she timidly asked him for her mother. He responded by hitting her. She remembers crying out in pain. Her father left without sending in her mother. Maria was left alone. Decades later while in therapy, Maria remembers feeling ashamed about needing her mother and embarrassed in front of her father. Additionally, she felt physical pain from being hit.

Notice that it never occurred to Maria that her parents could have done anything wrong. She internalized, instead, that it was her need for her mother that caused her pain, not her parent's inability to respond in a loving manner.

Neurochemically, let's examine what was happening to Maria. She first identified with a need for her mother. She was lonely and afraid, so her brain was experiencing a lack of serotonin and a heightened amount of adrenaline. When she encountered her father, who regularly hit Maria, she experienced more fear. Up goes the amount of adrenaline in her brain, and now add norepinephrine to the mix. Then her father hits her, causing her pain, sadness, and humiliation. Again, more adrenaline and norepinephrine are pumped into her system. At this point, her brain and body are overloaded with chemicals designed for fight or flight, neither of which she can do, and she is left alone to soothe herself. No one comes to comfort her or make sense of her father's unacceptable behavior.

Maria experienced many violations like this during her childhood. Her story illustrates the shame and pain that come from physical abuse. Her abuse occurred at the hands of her caregivers, so she also suffered a lack of "healing interactions." Her environment was not a safe place for a child. Her basic needs for comfort, connection, and safety were unmet. As a result, Maria internalized that her needs were not OK and grew up with a profound sense of shame that drove her into addiction at a young age.

Connection and Disconnection

When you are in a relationship that is healthy, you will consistently feel like a better person. The relationship seems to bring out the best in you. You think better, function better, and desire more connection with the world. It's helpful to look at your current relationships and see which ones give you the benefits of connection and which ones don't. No relationship is perfect. You may experience times of disconnection even in the most wonderful relationships. But it's useful to notice if connection or disconnection is the norm, and ask yourself why.

Dr. Judith Jordan and Cate Dooley put together the diagram on the following page to illustrate connection and disconnection.[10] Their work puts Dr. Miller's relational concepts into a helpful format.

A Word about Disconnection

As you look at the signs of disconnection, you may identify with them, even if you don't identify yourself as a sex and love addict. Chronic disconnection leads to depression, and depression is a common problem for many women. Disconnection is inevitable in a culture that places women in a one-down position to men.

Since families are products of culture–in fact, a family can be understood as a subculture–they inherit the same damaging beliefs about women. Mothers and daughters are caught within social and cultural agendas that play out in relationship with fathers and brothers and sons.

Sadly, families often pass on distorted ways of being in relationships with the opposite gender. This happens for women who are not necessarily sex and love addicts. It's important to make the following distinction: While most women know the pain of disconnection, not everyone who experiences disconnection is

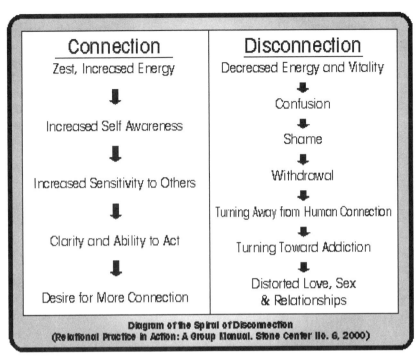

Diagram of the Spiral of Disconnection
(Relational Practice in Action: A Group Manual. Stone Center No. 6, 2000)

a sex and love addict. Also, not all childhood abuse results in sex and love addiction.

Neurochemistry and Addiction

When there is abuse in a family, there is psychological isolation. All abuse brings disconnection to a relationship, and if it's chronic, disconnection brings psychological isolation. Since one of the most terrifying human experiences is psychological isolation, chronic abuse creates terror. If chronic disconnection is the norm in a family, a child may turn to an addiction to take the place of a relationship. She uses a substance like food or a feeling like orgasm to soothe herself. Neurochemical changes in the brain while falling in love or becoming sexually aroused are measurable and powerful. For a young girl, these particular chemicals provide a new sense of well-being. She may accidentally discover pleasurable sensations that come from masturbation. Or she may find comfort with sweet food.

In Maria's case, she was masturbating every day by the age of five. She is not sure how she started masturbating, but when she did, she relied on it for comfort, for pleasure, and for its ability to help her fall asleep. Maria also escaped into fantasy. She imagined that some day, she would have love and a family of her own. Much like the Cinderella fairy tale, she imagined a man would rescue her from her unhappiness. Maria's use of masturbation and fantasy helped her survive the pain of her childhood. They also helped "soothe" her over-activated brain chemistry. They helped her block the shame she experienced in her childhood and numb the physical pain.

Like Maria, Heather also discovered masturbation as a child. She realized that the water jets in her parents' bathtub gave her pleasurable genital sensations that led to orgasm. She spent a lot of time in the bathroom masturbating as a child and recalls getting caught only once. Her father grew angry at the amount of time she was taking in the bathroom and entered uninvited to find her masturbating. He pulled her out of the tub and demanded that she never do it again. She didn't stop. She couldn't. Heather needed the consistent comfort masturbation offered her. It took the place of what she didn't receive in her family. In this way, we can see how masturbation became a necessary survival tool for Heather.

According to Carnes' research, most sex and love addicts come from families where there is emotional, physical, or sexual abuse in the home.[11] His survey shows the following numbers:

EMOTIONAL ABUSE: 97%

SEXUAL ABUSE: 81%

PHYSICAL ABUSE: 72%

Investigating early childhood can be extremely painful. Some women are surprised to discover that what they thought was normal didn't happen in other families. Maria says,

I thought all children were afraid of their parents. It was shocking to me when I learned my friends actually trusted their mothers or fathers. I envied them.

Why is it necessary to dig up the past? If it's going to hurt, what's the point? If you are experiencing symptoms of sex and love addiction, they will continue to get more painful until you are able to heal the original wound. The trauma of psychological isolation will keep you hostage. You cannot heal what you don't know.

If your early relationships were not safe places for relational development, it's likely that you learned to keep important parts of yourself hidden. You needed to feel loved. And you learned to do whatever possible to have this feeling.

In *The Drama of the Gifted Child,* Alice Miller illustrates this painful dilemma for girls raised in painful families:

[Girls] can be authentic and honest or they can be loved. If they chose to be themselves, they risk abandonment, emotionally or physically, by their parents. If they chose love, they abandon their true selves. Young girls will often prefer parental connection to anything else. Therefore, it is rare that a young girl or a woman elects to be true to herself rather than have a relationship.[12]

Like many women, you may not be aware of the despair you felt as a child. You may idealize your childhood, describing abuse as "not that bad" or minimizing it thinking "other people had it worse." You may have effectively adapted to the pain of isolation and abuse. You may be an expert at disguising pain, appearing confident when insecure, calm when afraid, tough when vulnerable, or angry when hurt. You may not even realize you're lonely. The loneliness that occurred in early development, however, has left deep wounds. The scar tissue around these wounds is thick. It's called denial. Denial successfully covers wounds, compassionately masking them from awareness.

Part of healing the isolation of your past is first identifying what happened. In addition to your current relationships, treatment for romantic addiction should contain an exploration of your early relationships. Who were your caretakers? What was your early physical, spiritual, economic, and emotional environment like? What are your earliest childhood memories? What losses did you suffer in childhood? What were the predominant feelings you remember having as a child? How was conflict handled in your home? As you explore, it's vital to remember that all forms of abuse are disconnections. Disconnections create fear. And chronic fear alters the brain. Having an addiction is not your fault. It's a way you learned to survive the pain of being afraid and alone.

What is Emotional Abuse?

Emotional abuse is foremost about isolation; a lack of nurturing, protection, and care that leads to emotional deprivation. Emotional abuse also occurs in many ways. Some of the following include:

- A significant caregiver doesn't allow a child to express feelings, or shames a child for having certain feelings.

A child searches for comfort after a difficult day at school. She comes to her mother with a tearful explanation about rejection from her friends. Her mother responds with, "What do you expect? That's the way girls act. You'll get over it." She doesn't feel comforted by her mother's words. Instead, she feels shame for having these feelings, and now also feels lonely and confused. She's less likely to trust talking with her mother next time.

A child frightened of the dark turns to his parents for comfort. His father shames him by saying "Quit acting like a girl. There's nothing to be afraid of." The boy learns fear isn't an emotion boys can have. He's left to handle his fear alone, and is also falsely raised to a status above girls. He will likely not share his fears in the future.

- When a child is forced to witness a caregiver's inappropriate expression of emotions, such as rage or terror, or is asked to take sides in marital problems.

In Tori's story, she experiences emotional abuse frequently. Tori witnessed her mother's suicide attempt and was exposed to her mother's emotional outburst toward her husband's mistress. There was no consideration for the impact this behavior had on Tori. Her mother could only focus on herself.

- When a parent expects perfection from a child.

Heather adapted to her feelings by becoming a quiet, compliant child in her family. She didn't want to disturb her mother and stepfather, and yet desperately needed their attention and focus. She grew accustomed to suppressing her feelings in an attempt to be what they desired her to be; she learned to stay out of the way. At the same time, she excelled in school because she received positive feelings listening to her parents talk about her academic achievements. She tried hard to do enough and be enough so that she could earn their love. But Heather's parents were emotionally unavailable to her, and couldn't respond to her valid needs for approval and unconditional love.

- Requiring a child to take on adult attributes too soon, such as caring for younger siblings.

Maggie was nine when her parents had a new baby. Sadly, her parents did not have a healthy marriage. Her father spent most of his time at work, and when he was home, he was tired and irritable. Maggie's mother was lonely and often took her frustration out on Maggie. She was critical and demanding. Maggie coped with her parents' moods by spending most of her time reading alone in her room.

After the birth of Maggie's baby brother, however, she could no longer retreat to her room. Maggie's mother began leaving home to see other men in an effort to deal with her loneliness. Maggie was left in charge of the new baby. She changed him, fed him, and put him to bed at night. Maggie remembers long afternoons, feeling angry and alone, and near tears with the huge responsibility of caring for her baby brother. She was still a child herself. Her own needs were not met. How could she meet the needs of a newborn?

Before the birth of her brother, Maggie was a lonely child. Her loneliness was compounded by adult responsibility she inherited at the tender age of nine. At twelve, Maggie began eating less. She avoided making friends at school and didn't have a boyfriend. She was emotionally hungry, and as she became increasingly burdened at home, she grew more physically hungry. She restricted her food in an attempt to control her feelings of loneliness and anger. Shortly after she left home for college, she dropped to such an unhealthy weight that she needed to be hospitalized.

Maggie's barren childhood is an example of emotional abuse. The absence of love and concern from her parents set her up for psychological isolation. Her eating disorder gave her a sense of control where she had none. It also mimicked the deprivation of her emotional life. Maggie's only comfort came from her moments alone, reading in her room. Maggie's lonely childhood left her starving for affection, guidance, and autonomy. She intensified her lack of love with a lack of food, further increasing her deprivation.

Maggie, now forty-one, has little experience with intimate connection. She learned early in her life that safety and comfort come from being alone, not from human relationships. Engulfed by adult responsibilities, Maggie learned that close relationships meant she would be taken advantage of and left behind. In this way, Maggie's family taught her to dread close relationships.

Maggie is now managing her eating disorder fairly well. If she's not attempting a romantic relationship, she feels hunger and eats. However, when she gets involved with someone romantically, her eating again becomes a problem, and she spirals into food deprivation Maggie struggles to be close to someone, but finds herself caught in a repetitive cycle of avoiding intimacy and closeness. In Chapter Six, a discussion of sexual anorexia will provide more insight into Maggie's cycle.

What is Sexual Abuse?

As a culture, our awareness of sexual abuse is growing, yet it is still common that women are not aware of the different types of sexual abuse they may have experienced. Overt forms of sexual abuse are usually easy to identify; these include actual physical penetration by an adult, which may or may not be intercourse. Fondling or masturbating a child, or having a child fondle or masturbate an adult is sexual abuse. Sexual kissing and hugging are also forms of overt sexual abuse, and are regularly identifiable for most adult women. Sexual abuse also includes being asked to exhibit yourself, or being exposed to pornography by adults or much older children.

Incest, or sexual abuse of a child by a relative or other person in a position of trust or authority, is a terrible violation of a child. A child molested by a stranger can run home for help or comfort. A victim of incest cannot. Incest offenders can be persons without direct blood or legal relationship to the child, such as a parent's lover, live-in nanny or housekeeper. Incest occurs between fathers and daughters, mothers and son, mothers and daughters, and fathers and sons. Grandparents, aunts, uncles, cousins, nieces, and nephews can all be incest offenders.

Covert Sexual Abuse

Covert sexual abuse is difficult for most women to identify. The word covert means "hidden." By its very nature, this form of abuse is difficult to understand. Covert sexual abuse, or emotional incest, happens when a parent uses a child to meet his or her emotional needs. The child feels responsible for the happiness and well-being of the parent. She may feel anxious, suffocated, inadequate, or aroused when with this parent. In *Silently Seduced,* Adams states,

Covert incest occurs when a child becomes the object of a parent's affections, love, passion, and preoccupation. The parent, motivated by the loneliness and emptiness created by a chronically troubled marriage or relationship, makes the child a surrogate partner. The boundary between caring and incestuous love is crossed when the relationship with the child exists to meet the needs of the parent rather than those of the child.[13]

Adams points to the risk of covert incest when adults are lonely in a marriage. We also see this dynamic when there is divorce or a single-parent situation. Adults raising children by themselves are vulnerable to loneliness, and as a result fall into the trap of thinking their children are there to meet their needs for companionship.

A father can sexualize a daughter by commenting on her body, the way she dresses, or by taking her special places with the intent to have her full attention. Mother's also sexualize their sons. Comments like "You will take care of Mommy, won't you?" or "Don't be like your father...", or "You're my handsome little man" create a dynamic between a mother and a son that is loaded with sexual energy.

The movie *The Prince of Tides,* based on a book by Pat Conroy, brilliantly illustrates the long-term effects of sexual abuse and trauma.[14] The children in the movie endure a horrible trauma when three men enter their home while their father is gone, and the mother and children are raped. But the children's mother prohibits them from ever discussing this tragedy with anyone. Not only does this prevent her children from finding a way to heal from this trauma, she also uses her son to fill the void she feels in her unhappy marriage.

As an adult, the character recalls his childhood with both exquisite bliss and torture of lying in bed with his mother as she held him and said, "You're my favorite." He now understands the pathological relationship he had with this mother, in addition to the trauma of rape, that has set him up for an inability to connect intimately with his own wife and daughters.

One of the best examples of father/daughter covert incest is in the movie *The Ballad of Jack and Rose.*[15] It's a story of a father living with his teenage daughter in isolation on a remote island in the Northeast. Since her mother left when she was a young girl, Rose cooks, cleans, and acts as a companion for her father. In fact, the father and daughter function more like a husband and wife. Rose supports Jack emotionally and he relies on her devotion. She doesn't attend school but learns from her father. In one scene, Jack and Rose nearly kiss. The intense sexual attraction scares Jack, sending him to the arms of another woman who lives in town. When Jack invites the woman, Kathleen, and her two teenage sons to live with them, Rose snaps. Upon discovering her father in bed with Kathleen, she tries to shoot her. Jack diffuses the situation, taking Rose into her bedroom, and the two share an intimate moment where Jack simply smiles at her and tucks her into bed. It's as if he enjoys his daughter's jealousy.

The relationship between Kathleen and Rose is complicated. Although Rose is starved for a mother figure, the bond she has with her father is so intense that she can't see Kathleen as anything but a rival. The drama escalates as Rose makes another attempt on Kathleen's life.

Rose also attempts to engage her father's jealousy by seducing Kathleen's son. Afterward, she hangs her virgin blood-stained sheet on the clothesline for her father to see. He's furious over her loss of sexual purity and attacks Kathleen's son in a fit of jealous rage. He soon sends Kathleen and her sons packing. Once again, father and daughter are alone.

Consequences of Covert Incest

Part of the pain of covert incest is the loss of relationship with the same-sex parent. The tension between Rose and Kathleen illustrates the friction between a mother and daughter when the primary emotional attachment for the father is with his daughter. Often, a mother grows jealous of the attention her spouse gives their daughter and, in turn, alienates her. In a family system, this is a profound abandonment for a young girl, who in essence loses both parents. One rejects her, while the other sexualizes her. In no way are her needs being met. She may feel used or trapped, which are the same feelings an overt incest survivor experiences.

Mostly, she will feel shame. Shame will result in psychological isolation. As an adult, she will exhibit symptoms of an covert incest survivor. Some of these may include:

- ▶ hasty entrance/exits in relationships
- ▶ difficulty saying "no"
- ▶ trouble with sexuality
- ▶ trouble identifying needs and wants
- ▶ excessive worry about others
- ▶ need for constant positive affirmation from others
- ▶ feeling suffocated by a romantic partner

It's imperative to note that covert incest carries with it a sense of being special, privileged or unique. The chosen child experiences confusion that comes with feeling special and shameful at the same time. She may also feel guilty for wanting her mother out of the picture when her father is around. A covert incest survivor is given certain privileges that are meant only for adults. She may, as a result, feel superior to other children or teenagers her age. Her special status as "Daddy's girl" creates difficulty for her in identifying this type of relationship as abusive. For this reason, covert incest is problematic for an adult woman. It's difficult to name and, therefore, the effects can go on for a long time, often ruining a woman's sexual and relational life without her having any idea why.

As an adult, marriage or a close relationship may feel suffocating. She'll frequently blame her partner when there is relational difficulty, never seeing how wounded she is or finding the help she needs. Additionally, women who are covert incest survivors frequently find they have trouble parenting. They often see their daughters as rivals and suffer shame for these feelings.

Barbara

Barbara remembers a painful Thanksgiving holiday when she and her mother were preparing the table for dinner. When her father entered the room, she went to greet him and her mother said, "I'm going to lose my husband to my daughter." Barbara remembers feeling a combination of shock, humiliation and fear…fear that she had been caught. She felt her mother knew that deep inside, she only wanted her father for herself. She wanted her mother as far away as possible.

As Barbara grew, she was profoundly disconnected from her mother. The lack of maternal attachment affected her adult female relationships. She preferred men to women, and alienated women with her arrogance and detachment. She always felt superior to women. Her grandiosity was a cover for the deep emptiness and self-hatred she felt inside. Her mother's rejection taught her to reject herself.

Gender Confusion

Maria experienced complications as an adult in both male and female relationships. With men, she vacillated between being intensely sexual or cold and unyielding. With women, she developed intense feelings, either quickly disregarding them, or idolizing and pursuing a close relationship. At one point after her divorce, Maria thought she might be a lesbian, and even pursued a sexual relationship with a woman. Maria's experience is common for victims of covert incest that have been abandoned by a same-sex parent. They crave the affection of their gender, which is an unconscious replacement for a mother, and suffer confusion about what this longing means. We will discuss mother hunger in more detail in Chapter Nine.

Emotional incest can also happen between a parent and a same-sex child. A mother can use her daughter to meet her needs for connection rather than friends her own age, confiding in her daughter about her marriage or life that are not appropriate. Likewise, a father can become enmeshed with his son, thereby failing to allow his son to develop age-appropriate relationships. These children will find relationships with the same gender particularly complicated as adults. They may experience confusion with their sexual preference as well.

Gender Rage

When a daughter has been sexualized by her father, she often feels torn between pleasure and anger. The combination creates a toxic mix. As an adult, if these feelings are not made conscious and healed, she will act them out. Some women carry a deep hatred for men while at the same time are sexually aroused by them. Others feel no sexual desire for men, but angrily pursue them to gain power or financial gain. These forms of erotic rage will be further discussed in Chapter Six.

Jane

Jane has memories of her father watching her intensely as she entered puberty and developed breasts. She can remember his eyes fixated on her in the kitchen. She also remembers spotting him watching her undress in her bedroom. Once, he even commented about her breasts, "Wow where did you get those? Definitely not from your mother!" Jane could feel the sting of the insult directed at her mother, and didn't know how to make sense of her own pride in being recognized as a woman.

It felt good to be noticed by him, but it also felt creepy. I could never look him in the face when he said things like that to me.

Jane also remembers her father coming home from work, and instead of greeting her mother, coming to her first. She didn't like this intense focus from him. "I just wanted him to go back to work."

Jane's experience with her father's inappropriate sexual comments, and boundaries illustrates the unique pain of covert sexual abuse. Some of the abuse feels good, while at the same time produces shame. She enjoyed being noticed, yet her father's comments about her breasts and his voyeuristic behavior also left her feeling icky. The "ick" feeling is a sign of shame. Jane took on the shame her father should have felt. We can see her shame in her inability to look at her father in the eye and the "creepy" feeling she remembers. Understanding Jane's childhood sheds light on her sexual behavior as an adult. She's been a dancer in strip club for a number of years. Jane feels disgust toward the men who come to the club. Her feelings, in part, are left over from the feelings she had toward her father as a developing young woman. She hasn't been able to identify or heal this trauma in therapy, so she repeats her trauma every night dancing for strangers.

Jane is aware that she enjoys control and power at her job. She's reacting to the powerlessness she felt as a young girl in her home. She couldn't stop her father's behavior, nor did she have power over her situation. At work, she feels more in control because she chooses this work and is being paid. In time, as she heals, she may reconsider how much of her work is actually a choice, or perhaps an automatic repetition of her childhood.

What is Physical Abuse?

Physical abuse includes most things we easily identify as abuse–slapping, hitting, shaking, biting, pulling hair, and spanking. Physical abuse also includes tickling a child into hysteria, or witnessing others being hit, such as a sibling or parent. Lack of appropriate touch is also a form of physical abuse. Brooklyn recalls her upbringing as unaffectionate.

My parents weren't hugging types…we were never tucked in at night, or offered hugs if we were hurt. I do remember one time when I was very little. I had the flu. My mom sat by the side of my bed and stroked my arm for a few minutes. It was the best feeling. I didn't want her to stop.

As an adult, Brooklyn's lovers offer her much-needed touch. Part of her recovery will involve healing her touch deprivation. She will be encouraged to get regular, non-sexual massages to heal her unmet need for touch. She will begin to learn to ask appropriate people for a hug when she needs it.

For Maria, touch was also a complicated issue. Not only had her family shown a lack of affection and tenderness, spankings were common, brutal, and terrifying. Witnessing her sister's beatings was equally traumatizing. As an adult, her touch deprivation had an element of terror with it. She recoiled from the slightest offer of affection from people. Her friends often thought of her as "cold and distant…aloof." Yet, with her lovers, she could be intensely sexual. She learned early in life to get her touch needs met through sexual activity. Maria explained in therapy,

I don't really like sex. I'm not sure why I am having so much of it…I hardly ever have an orgasm and, afterward, I usually feel lonely.

Although Maria uncovered many reasons for her sexual behavior in therapy, one element of sexual craving is touch deprivation resulting from childhood physical abuse and neglect. In an effort to heal her body's need for touch, she craved sex, even though it wasn't satisfying or nurturing for her.

Abuse and Boundaries

When a child is young, she's vulnerable. She depends on her caregivers for support, food, life, and security. If she's abused, she becomes too vulnerable. She can't protect herself. As a result, vulnerability means loss of self, devastation, and powerlessness. She learns to compensate by forming walls, becoming extremely accommodating, or both. She has difficulty saying "no" or knowing what she desires. She develops a faulty system of boundaries. According to Pia Melody:

A damaged boundary system has holes in it. People with damaged boundaries can at times or with certain individuals say "no," set limits, and take care of themselves. At other times or with other people, they are powerless to set boundaries....for example, a person may be able to set boundaries with everyone but authority figures, or her spouse, or her child.[16]

Melody makes the distinction between a damaged boundary system, and a "nonexistent" boundary system. In the non-existent system, a woman has no ability to say no under any circumstances, and cannot identify "being abused or being abusive."[17]

In Maria's case, she was often afraid as a child. She learned she couldn't trust anyone. In her family, she formed a personality that vacillated between tough and intimidating to seductive and child-like. Her armored personality covered a hurt little girl. Her boundaries were sometimes weak and ambiguous, other times rigid and tight.   Her sexual behavior masked the fear and dread she felt about being close to someone while still allowing her the illusion of love and access to human touch. Until Maria faced her childhood abuse, she couldn't risk bonding with anyone.

Signs of Damaged Boundaries

All forms of abuse are boundary violations. Consistent boundary violations in childhood create adults who do not have healthy ways of staying protected while in close relationship with others. The result is a fractured ability to be available for intimacy. What are some signs of damaged boundaries?

- touching someone without permission
- inability to say no to physical or sexual contact
- answering sexual questions or discussing sexuality at inappropriate times
- accepting blame for other's feelings or problems
- allowing others to direct your life and make your choices
- acting impulsively, and violating your own personal values to make a partner happy
- flirting indiscriminately as a way of being relational
- risky sexual practices, such as sex without protection or with unfamiliar partners
- accepting food and gifts you don't want; eating when you're not hungry but someone else wants you to
- explaining your behavior when a simple "no" would be enough
- expecting someone else to anticipate your desires or needs and fulfill them
- extreme isolation
- self-abuse

Strangers to Connection: Love and Sex Addicts

A child will go through amazing psychological gymnastics to avoid the pain of psychological isolation. For a child, loneliness feels like death. When children experience terrifying isolation, they think it's their fault. Psychological isolation creates shame and a belief that "something is wrong with me." A child will seek an emotional escape to numb or deny this kind of terror and pain. One very successful way to do this is with an addiction. Addiction alters the brain. It replaces the "feel good" hormones that were compromised during trauma.

Carnes gives us another definition of addiction. He calls it "a failure to bond."[18] What he means is the addiction takes the place of a human bond. In this way, addiction becomes a relationship. In essence, addiction replaces human connection. It does what true connection should have done. Remember from Chapter One: Addiction is a love relationship. It becomes the primary bond. With an increased understanding of family and cultural trauma, we can see how an addiction substitutes for the warmth and pleasure of a loving relationship.

After reading this chapter, you may be examining your own trauma history. In doing so, be gentle with yourself. These are difficult issues. Keep in mind that if you have suffered like the women in our stories, your brain is not always going to behave as your friend. You have found a way to survive your compromised brain chemistry. You have an addiction. The addiction gives you some of the "feel good" hormones that your brain is missing from exposure to trauma.

In order to heal your brain, however, you will not be able to continue to use your addiction to feel OK. The brain will stay attached to the chemicals of sex and love and never allow you to "bond" intimately with another person.

Chapter Four
A Painful Paradox

*Yet a vague but persistent nagging within our deepest self continued to bear wit-
ness that all was not well. Despite all the cultural and rational camouflage
behind which our addiction could hide, it was impossible, short of suicide, to kill
that innermost voice that whispered to us of life's opportunities for growth and
wholeness that we were helplessly letting slip by...that of having left life unlived,
of having turned our backs on the possibility of fulfilling a meaningful destiny.*
Sex and Love Addicts Anonymous[1]

Love and sex addicts are caught in a painful paradox resulting from two co-exist-
ing realities: the need for an intimate relationship and a terror of close connection. The body has internalized that human connection as traumatic so the search
for love collides with fear. When you are romantically involved with someone,
you repeatedly find yourself spiraling between periods of intense pleasure and
unbearable isolation. The endorphins released in the body during lovemaking,
orgasm, or while falling in love connect to the pleasure center in the brain. In this
sense, sexual arousal can be intoxicating. It can also serve to numb or block pain.
You may find the mind-altering effects of romance or orgasm necessary to feel
happy. Without a relationship–or the pursuit of one–life seems empty and void
of pleasure.

Over time, this pattern creates extreme fatigue and despair. You grow weary.
At times, it feels like you're drowning. A haze of despair covers your daily activities and everything takes too much effort. Certain unwanted personality traits
plague you–procrastination, ambivalence, confusion, irritability, and boredom.
Like other drugs, sex and love addiction is a way to medicate painful feelings. It's
a way to feel in control of oneself or others. Sex and love become commodities
to be used to alter reality and feel better. Ultimately, the addiction creates pain
and despair. Sex and love addiction, therefore, can be understood as a method of
self-abuse.

Control, Fear, and Shame

Sex and love addiction is not about either love or sex. It is about control, fear,
and shame. If you find yourself addicted to relationships, your hidden fears and
shame are driving your relational behaviors. You will consciously or unconsciously work to control someone else's behavior or ideas about you in an effort

to secure love. To avoid abandonment or engulfment, love gets twisted into emotional quicksand.

Control: Efforts to control yourself can include plastic surgery, geographical moves, career changes, having more children/no children, etc. Efforts to control your partner range from constantly needing to know where he/she is, withholding finances, withholding affection and sex, or making all the decisions about the relationship.

Fear: Fear prevents you from being emotionally accessible to another person. You learn to hide your authentic feelings in an effort to protect yourself from being hurt. Think of it like a turtle–you carry a shell to protect the tender parts of yourself. On the outside, you may seem strong and confident, but inside, you feel like a young girl who is terrified of being abandoned, hurt, and rejected.

Shame: The shame from cultural beliefs and childhood wounds prevent you from knowing your worth. Growing up lonely and frightened teaches you that you aren't loveable. You develop the ability to compartmentalize your personality in an effort to separate parts of yourself that others don't like. Compartmentalization creates more disconnection, and disconnection produces shame.

Miranda

Miranda learned at a young age to be sexy. She remembers her father coaching her to be sexual, explaining that if he had been a woman, he would have been a whore. Miranda couldn't see how inappropriate her father's behavior was. She was grateful for his attention and thought it was love. She remembers being asked to shower with him as a young girl, and being eye level with his penis.

When she relates this story in therapy, she has no feeling attached to it. She reports the story as if it happened to someone else. She even giggles a bit. Miranda is new to therapy and is recently sober from drug addiction. She's only beginning to examine her sex and love addiction. Miranda describes her sexuality openly in therapy.

I have sex like a man. I just want to get off and then leave. I like sex with couples because it feels great to have two people wanting me, and I like anonymous sex. Watching porn is necessary for me to feel sexual with my partner.

Miranda is not yet aware of how she uses sex to escape the fear of intimacy. She discusses sex as if it's a device to be used to make herself feel better. Nowhere in her vocabulary does sex involve mutuality or respectful sharing. In fact, she seems unaware of her impact on others. Miranda recently experienced a breakthrough in her therapeutic work when her boyfriend told her she was too demanding and needy and that he didn't feel sexually attracted to her anymore.

Incidentally, Miranda had put on a great deal of weight during their relationship, which he said was the reason he found her sexually "disgusting."

Miranda came to therapy after this encounter feeling grief, fear, and desperation. She said she had a desire to use drugs again. While exploring her feelings of rejection, she tearfully admitted to a pattern with food that happened each time she had a boyfriend. In relationships, she gained weight, and when single, she lost weight.

When her therapist asked her to think about what her weight was trying to tell her, she grew very still. Within moments, she came into contact with the rage she had been carrying toward her father, who always tried to coach her to look and dress a certain way, and maintain a certain body weight. She exclaimed, "I can eat whatever I want!" With further exploration, Miranda could see the rebelliousness that her eating represented. Food gave her a sense of power, and eating secretly made her feel in control of her choices.

Miranda's sexual and eating behaviors are causing her problems. While she seems clear about what kind of sex she likes and how she wants to have it, she isn't happy in her relationships. She weighs 70 pounds more than her healthy weight. She's bored and tired at work, and frequently finds herself irritable and rageful with her boyfriend. She is ambivalent about the relationship and whether or not it's right for her.

Part of her confusion is related to the fact that she is financially supporting him. On a deep level, she feels she must buy love. She doesn't trust her own worth. Miranda's fear and shame keeps her trapped in a cycle of control; using sex and money to secure love and a relationship. Without self-awareness, acceptance and love, she won't be able to let go of these three painful attributes. She won't know authentic connection and intimacy.

While Miranda is a long way from sobriety, either with food or sex, she is reaching insight and awareness that will help her as she continues her journey toward wellness. She has used many addictions to escape her painful reality: drugs, food, and sex. In therapy, she will learn what she's trying to avoid and put measures in place to help her stay present to her reality rather than compulsively avoid it.

Bonded to Sex and Love

As we discussed in Chapter One, addiction is a love relationship. The addiction becomes the primary bond in a woman's life. For a sex and love addict, a bond forms with the experience of being in love or being sexual instead of with a person. Imagine how confusing this can be. It is the high of falling in love or becoming aroused that the brain attaches to. This allows you to leave a relationship when it no longer seems to "work" and find a new one without feeling much sadness over a particular person.

Or perhaps no one seems to generate enough neurochemistry for you to "fall in love." It seems like you just can't find the "right" person. Or maybe you are disturbed about your inability to let go of a particularly destructive relationship.

You can't understand why even though your partner was unreliable, irritable, moody, and demanding, you still miss the relationship.

As with any drug, sex and love will eventually stop providing the "high" necessary to feel normal. Relationships become empty, dark, and void of anything rewarding. You may routinely feel your partners don't know you enough, don't want you enough, and don't understand you enough. You are consumed with insecurity and overcome with a spiritual bankruptcy that robs you from feeling peaceful and joyful. The following patterns may emerge:

- increased fear or hopeless during periods of separation from the relationship
- lack of trust that your partner is faithful or can handle your needs
- craving more sex or shutting down sexually
- changes in eating and/or spending patterns
- increased use of alcohol or other addictive substances.
- frequent nightmares that leave you feeling insecure and panicked
- times of extreme anxiety or panic when pursuing ambitions
- increased isolation from friends and hobbies that used to bring pleasure
- dampened desire for life that may manifest as depression

It takes considerable effort to determine that one is using romance addictively. Often in order for this awareness to take place, a woman will first find herself terribly broken and alone. When these painful patterns become intolerable, before she seeks help, a woman may try leaving her current relationship for a new one, secretly act out sexually to tolerate the pain, shut down her sexual desire, or become demanding and alienate her partner. Her choices are many. Sadly, however, they are part of a cycle that will take her further from herself and further into the addictive system. The addiction becomes a method of self-abuse.

What is the Addictive System?

Carnes developed the Addictive System to provide an understanding of behavior that is repetitive, predictable, and powerful. Every addiction, whether to a substance or a process, follows this powerful cycle. It's helpful to understand the nature of the addictive system. For one, it is cyclical. Without intervention, the cycle continues despite negative consequences.

Without a break in the cycle, the addictive system will gain power and momentum, eventually taking over your life. In order to better understand the cyclical, nature of addiction, we have provided an illustration of Carnes' addictive system.[2] Additionally, we describe each component of the cycle.

Belief System

The illustration of the addictive system starts with basic core beliefs. These beliefs are largely unconscious. They generally show up when a woman begins therapy or 12-step meetings. As we outlined in Chapter Two, there are four

The Addictive System

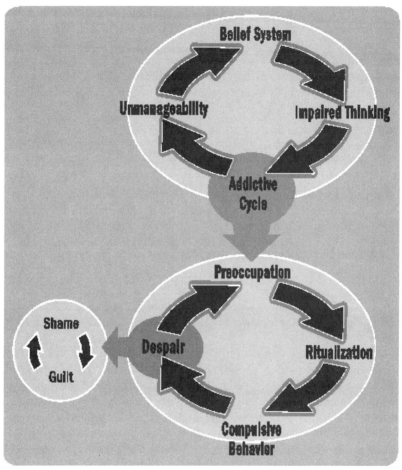

©2994 The Addictive System, Dr. Patrick Carnes, Ph.D.

beliefs common to each addict:

- I am basically a bad, unworthy person.
- No one would love me as I am.
- My needs are never going to be met if I have to depend on others.
- Sex is my most important need, or most important sign of love, or most terrifying need.

These painful beliefs make up the core of an addiction–shame. Shame is the unbearable feeling of being unworthy of connection. It's the feeling of being shut out of connection because something about you is defective. It's the belief that you are not capable of changing this fact. Shame leads to loneliness, and as we discussed in Chapter Three, traumatic loneliness and lack of bonding leads to addiction. Humans cannot bear isolation. Therefore, you crave a "fix."

Using sex, love or romance soothes the starving brain. The solution brings the illusion of connection. One of the greatest pains of sex and love addiction is the betrayal–the loss of the dream that a relationship will foster your happiness, growth, and wholeness. The one thing that used to work, should work, everyone says works, fails to do so. When sex and love are addictive the illusion of connection eventually crumbles, and loneliness grows deeper and more profound.

Impaired Thinking

The system works like this: something triggers your negative core beliefs and your brain is off and running. Impaired thinking sets in. Impaired thinking feels like normal thinking for you. It's the way you see the world. Most impaired thinking is automatic and unconscious. It distorts reality and creates a need for escape. The thoughts are unbearable. Impaired thinking creates an environment fertile for compulsive behavior.

For example, Maria's impaired thinking included thoughts and judgments about men. She believed men had no feelings, so she could minimize any impact her behavior might cause. She seemed unaware that men were able to experience pain so she justified her flirtation and seduction. Additionally, Maria had internalized Cultural Belief Number Three, thinking, that if she was sexually desirable, she would earn love. She told herself that serving men sexually was what she was designed to do.

Like most addicts, Maria's impaired thinking allowed her to swing from a dark feeling of insecurity to a heady sense of being larger than life. Her sense of insecurity fueled her need for male affirmation, and her grandiosity allowed her to leave relationships with no remorse. The St. Augustine Big Book of sex and love addicts anonymous illustrates impaired thinking in the following way:

Indeed, our sex and love addiction, dictating who and what we had striven to be in the world, had supplied our principal source of identity, our entire self-concept. We had felt so self-assured, surveying a crowded room, advertising our availability. We knew we would be met with similar energy from others, a never-ending source of "rainchecks." What security we had derived, knowing we could foster insecurity in others, making them all the more needy and dependent on us, thus insuring our own sense of well-being. We enjoyed the power our sex appeal gave us...we felt safe in knowing that physically, emotionally, and mentally we could continue to attract new people to us....[3]

Preoccupation

In the preoccupation stage of the cycle, a woman is unable to endure the pain of impaired thinking. The brain switches quickly to something consuming in order to block the pain of her negative beliefs. When you're in the preoccupation stage, you're involved in repetitive thinking. You can become obsessed in myriad ways. You might be at work, completing a certain task, but your mind is elsewhere. The following list includes a few places your mind could go in the preoccupation stage of the cycle. Time thinking about:

- a lover
- lovemaking
- satisfying a partner
- visiting chat rooms, viewing pornography or reading erotica
- going to a bar to find a sexual opportunity
- where/when to masturbate
- not having sex
- a lover's whereabouts

Clearly, preoccupation steals time. Preoccupation is all-consuming. It distracts you from work or family, and leaves your mind full of urgent thoughts. Obsession floods the brain with hormones that are sometimes uplifting, sometimes angering, and usually energizing. It's a way to medicate negative emotions without anyone knowing. It's a way to feel in control. Obsession and preoccupation are powerful narcotics. Without intervention, you may not realize you're medicating yourself with these urgent thoughts.

Ritualization

There are rituals that accompany any addiction. For a person addicted to cigarettes, the ritual includes the unwrapping of a new pack of cigarettes, pouring a cold drink, lighting the cigarette, and taking the first inhale. Starbucks has figured out the ritual for coffee drinkers–dark, cozy environments, familiar sounds of cappuccino machines, creative, colorful flavor options, and convenient, trendy locations near businesses and shopping. For the marijuana user the ritual involves rolling of the joint, licking the paper, and the initial inhale.

For a sex and love addict, rituals are many. They include grooming activity, such as shopping for the right outfit, dressing provocatively, and listening to arousing music before going out to a bar or having a lover to dinner. Rituals around pornography involve the right props: towels, lotions, or sex toys. The rituals are very important to the addict as they provide comfort, consistency, and the illusion of control. They give the addict the idea that everything is OK. They also serve to induce a trance-like state. In this condition, a woman has an altered sense of reality. She's less aware of her choices and their consequences.

Jane

In therapy, Jane recalls the first time she received money for a sexual encounter. She detailed the lingerie she purchased and the dress she wore. She described the incredible adrenaline that coursed through her veins as she drove to meet the man to have sex.

It was as if time stood still. I couldn't believe I was doing this. Part of me knew it was incredibly risky, even dangerous, but I was also thrilled and aroused. It's like I was on automatic pilot. I felt powerful and scared at the same time.

Compulsive Behavior

Sexuality is core to our personhood. It's the center of our soul. When we're sexual, we share ourselves. Our sexual expression tells a story about who we are. When we like who we are, the way we express ourselves sexually shows a deep respect for the individuality of another, the sacredness of ourselves, and the beauty of a sexual encounter. The legacy of physical, emotional, or sexual abuse damages the core self, however, and sexuality becomes distorted.

When sex is part of a bruised self, many survivors of child abuse discover that their sexuality becomes addictive. Compulsive romantic behavior–whether extreme sexual avoidance, obsessive devotion to a destructive relationship, or unbridled promiscuity–is an overt clue there's a problem.

The American Heritage Dictionary defines compulsion as "an irresistible impulse to act, regardless of the rationality of the motivation."[4] This definition helps us understand that when someone behaves sexually in ways that are self-destructive, the motivation behind the actions doesn't have to make sense. The motivation isn't logical. Brooklyn describes the insanity of sex addiction beautifully. With dark circles under her eyes, and sadness in her voice, she details a romantic binge with her husband saying, "I snorted a line of Ray this weekend, and I'm paying for it today."

In the cycle of sex and love addiction, sexual and romantic behavior reveals your brokenness. You can disown your sexuality, or use it to gain a sense of power. In this way, your body becomes a separate commodity to be dismissed or used. You may find yourself compelled to action despite negative, painful consequences. At this point in the cycle, you cannot stop. You cannot say "no." Some women make efforts to change their acting-out behaviors. Oftentimes, these attempts are something like an alcoholic vowing not to drink. She may make it a few days, or hours, even months only to return to the familiar drug. One nineteen-year-old explained her efforts like this:

After I was expelled from school, I stopped acting out for awhile. I stayed away from the strip clubs and from most of the men I knew. But I missed it all. I missed the power. Nowhere else in my life did I feel that good. So I went back. But this time, it was more dangerous. It's as if the time I was away made my need stronger. It wasn't enough to strip. I wanted to take men home with me. I got scared.

Despair

As the cycle repeats over days, months, or years, the initial feelings of energy and "high" wear off. You find yourself feeling despair. By this point, you may face a number of negative consequences, which may include terminated pregnancies,

STDs, divorce(s), loss of income, financial insecurities, unwanted children, fatigue, weakened immune system functioning, depression, damaged dreams, or the loss of friends. Sometimes, you may feel it would be easier to die than continue living with this loneliness and shame.

Unmanageability

In the addictive system, your life eventually spins out of control. The amount of time this takes is different for each woman. You'll see from our stories that some women intervene on the cycle in their late teens or early twenties, some in their thirties and some not until forties, fifties, or even sixties. There is no right or wrong time to start treating the addiction. It's about what you can tolerate. It's about when you determine your life is out of control. In 12-step circles, this is called unmanageability. Unmanageability means the addiction has consumed your life. The only thing that matters is the next fix. The only thing that feels like living is the addiction. You may go through the motions of working, being married or parenting, however, you're not really there.

Since your addiction is the only thing that makes you feel alive, you're constantly on edge, waiting for the next "hit." If left untreated, addiction grows. Each time you act out after time "on the wagon," you become more creative, more daring, and more risky. And each time you feel more defective, broken, and lost. Sadly, these feelings support your original belief system: *I am basically a bad, unworthy person, and no one would love me if they knew me.* And the cycle of self-abuse starts again.

Self-Development and Addiction

Eventually, unmanageability, despair, and shame may jolt you out of denial. If the addictive cycle goes on for years, the jolt must be strong enough to get your attention. Violence and pain are too frequently part of hitting bottom and waking up. For example, a woman out at night seeking a sexual partner finds herself against a wall with a knife at her throat. Or the relationship that only periodically became violent escalates with a trip to the hospital. One client attempted suicide to get her husband's attention. In therapy, she explained, "I didn't want to die...I just wanted him to know how much his cheating had hurt me."

Much time, energy, and research has contributed to our current understanding of addiction. We know addictions carry negative consequences involving finances, health, and safety. They grow in intensity and power. Although addictions create problems, many stay in addictive habits because they soothe the brain. Addictions may permit a temporary freedom from the dark abyss, but there is a cost. When you use an addiction to escape pain, you also escape knowing yourself. If sex and love addiction is your drug of choice, you are in love with the illusion of love. In the words of the St. Augustine Fellowship,

... through sex, charm, emotional appeal or persuasive intellect, we had used other people as "drugs" to avoid facing our own personal inadequacy.[5]

Addictive relationships serve to keep you separate from becoming a whole person. Your double life freezes personal development and you cannot truly know yourself. You trade yourself for the drug. In this way, addictions provide an escape from reality and an escape from the self.

Chapter Five
Understanding Compulsive
Romantic Behavior

*The Romantic is addicted to ecstasy–and her yearning for rapture becomes agony
as she realizes the insatiability of her desire. Seeking absolute union she comes
upon the pain of separation. And feeling unable to bear this pain, she longs to
forget. Thus, ultimately, the longing for merger (addiction) becomes the longing
to forget...the addiction actually helps the addict forget for a while by drawing
her into unconsciousness. But eventually the addict needs more and more to forget, so much that the addictive substance or activity ceases to help. Instead, it
turns her back upon herself in agony.*

Linda S. Leonard, *Witness to the Fire*[1]

Compulsive behavior is a way to avoid being close to another person. It's a way
to hide from feelings that you find unpleasant or shameful, such as dependency,
sadness, anger, or fear. Understood in this way, compulsive behavior can be seen
as a strategy of escape. Compulsive behavior permits you to be in a relationship
while keeping parts of yourself separate. You remain emotionally inaccessible,
and in this way you don't see reality clearly. It's a method of separateness born
from a need for protection. Strategies of escape allow you to present a picture of
being intimate, while in fact, you aren't.

You may play a role: a good wife, a busy mother, an active business woman,
or an erotic temptress. In reality, however, you have one foot in the relationship
and one foot out. You don't know if this relationship is the one you want or if it's
good for you. You may feel dependent–or incredibly attracted to your partner–yet
maintain a nagging suspicion that something is missing or something is wrong.

Compulsive Behavior: Escaping Intimacy

A woman is hardwired for connection. If connection is not happening, she'll create the illusion of connection. In order to do this, she will develop strategies of
escape that allow her to adapt to the relationship. What are some ways to adapt
to unhealthy relationships? Some women begin using substances while others
stay frantically busy to avoid loneliness. The following list highlights some common adaptations women compulsively use to stay in unhealthy relationships.

- being compliant and nice rather than truthful and real
- lying and keeping secrets
- talking non-stop to maintain the appearance of connection
- misusing food to medicate unpleasant or shameful emotions
- abusing substances to hide from painful feelings (prescription medication, illegal drugs, alcohol, food, and/or nicotine)
- working too much, creating chronic fatigue and unavailability
- creating financial problems through over-spending, and/or hoarding
- staying busy to generate intensity outside the relationship and avoid connection
- using sarcasm in conversation. The literal definition of sarcasm is "tearing flesh."
- playing the victim/martyr to gain connection through pity
- having affairs, both emotional and sexual
- choosing partners repeatedly who are emotionally unavailable

As humans, we all disconnect from ourselves and others periodically. Our connections with others are not always warm and affirming, so occasionally we find ourselves needing a time out, or hiding our vulnerability in an effort to feel more secure. Disconnecting doesn't necessarily indicate that you have an addiction. You have an addiction when you can no longer control when or how you escape the relationship. Your need for separation becomes out of your control. You don't simply take a few minutes to cool off from a conflict or during an intimate moment.

Instead, you habitually create drama in order to escape your partner, or you emotionally abandon the relationship with other pursuits. You may find yourself going through the motions of a relationship without really being there. Compulsive strategies of escape are different from normal time-outs because they become chronic and painful. Addictive strategies of escape destroy intimacy and solitary efforts to change them aren't effective.

When Escaping Intimacy Becomes Addictive

How do you determine if your escape strategies are addictive? One way to identify an addictive need to escape is to notice if you do it even when you don't want to. For example, you may remember Heather and Maria who both found themselves compulsively leaving relationships. Maria left her marriage even though she hated the idea of divorce. Maria had learned to bond with sex as a sign that a man loved her, so when her marriage became sexually complicated, she didn't know what to do and no longer felt loved.

Like Maria, Heather found herself broken and lost when her ability to disconnect from a relationship became habit. Early on Heather enjoyed her ability to stay unavailable in relationships. It gave her a sense of power.

However, she grew afraid when her desire for a committed relationship began to compete with her ability to stay detached. She decided to find help when she broke off a relationship with a man she deeply cared for. Her behavior was out of her control.

You may also remember Maggie from an earlier chapter. She learned to escape her painful childhood by retreating into her room, reading books and, eventually, she developed an eating disorder to manage her pain. Now a grown woman in her mid-forties who is steadily recovering from her eating disorder, Maggie describes her desperate wish for a partner and a family. But her child-hood patterns of isolating formed strong neural connectors in her brain. She developed strategies to avoid connection, not build connection.

It's horribly frustrating for Maggie when her desire for romantic connection is automatically thwarted by her brain chemistry. Her brain registers fear and moves into flight when a relationship becomes intimate. She feels irritable if the relationship grows too close. She finds things wrong with her lover, judges him, and withdraws from him. Her responses are automatic and happen outside her control.

She learned to avoid intimacy in her family, and these early patterns are set in her brain. She must create new neural pathways that enable her to connect with others. This is a difficult process and requires much support and time. Although Maggie's patterns are different from Maria's and Heather's, the underlying issues are the same. These women do not feel safe being intimate and find ways to escape their relationships. Maggie's situation is showing signs of an addiction. It may be helpful at this point to remember the criteria for addiction:

- ▶ loss of time with family members and friends
- ▶ an experience of being "high" followed by secrecy and shame
- ▶ negative consequences, which may include health problems and financial problems
- ▶ obsessive preoccupation with the relationship or sex
- ▶ attempts to stop your behavior or obsession bring considerable irritability and distress
- ▶ behavior becomes riskier or more intense

Maggie has tried to stop her isolating behavior without success. She grows irritable when intimacy becomes challenging in a relationship, and she finds herself preoccupied with her situation. She makes repeated attempts to find a healthy relationship, only to find herself alone again. Her despair and shame are growing. Maggie's addiction to isolation is called sexual anorexia. While sexual anorexia looks different from other forms of sexual addiction, the common escape from human connection is the unifying thread. We will explore this further in Chapter Six.

Uncovering the Beliefs Behind Compulsive Romantic Behavior

If sex and love addiction is no longer bringing you enough pleasure to mask the pain of loneliness and shame, you're ready to explore the beliefs that fuel your romantic behavior. It's helpful to keep in mind, however, that you have learned these beliefs over a lifetime. They are patterned into your being. For most women, their sex and love addiction developed in early childhood and adolescence in response to negative core beliefs. As a result, becoming *aware* of the negative beliefs will not stop them from sabotaging your attempts to find close relationships. As you become more aware of the ways you avoid intimacy, you will see how much they have become part of who you are. This is often a painful first step toward recovering your original self–the self you were meant to be.

Although awareness is a necessary beginning to the healing process, it involves more than knowing your behavior is not working. Awareness means learning that your addictive behavior makes your negative beliefs stronger. The more you act compulsively, the more power your faulty thinking has over your life. The more you act compulsively, the more you believe that you're not worthy of love.

As your compulsive behavior grows, so does the feeling that you can't trust anyone. The more you try to rely only on yourself for answers, the more isolated you become. Damaged thinking distorts who you are. It poisons your sexuality and your romantic relationships. Recall the beliefs that Carnes identified for women addicted to sex and love. The following beliefs about sexuality are not true, but they are powerful. They are not always conscious, yet they direct romantic behavior.

▶ Sex is my most important need.
▶ Sex is my most important sign that someone loves me.
▶ Sex is my most terrifying need.

Carnes' beliefs knit their way into each of the four cultural beliefs that we outlined in Chapter Two.

▶ I must be good to have love.
▶ I am not really a woman unless someone desires me sexually or romantically.
▶ If I am sexual, I am bad.
▶ I must be sexual to have love.

You may notice that the four cultural beliefs are similar to one another. While this is the case, they also hold important contradictions which set you up for a double bind. A double bind is a distortion of reality that exists when following either rule or belief sets you up to fail. For example, if you must be "good to have love" (Cultural Belief Number One) and yet to be sexual means you are "bad" (Cultural Belief Number Three), you cannot be sexual and also have a loving relationship. While this makes no logical sense, the cultural beliefs are powerful and make intimate relationships very difficult.

Double binds make you crazy and confused. They are the fuel for compulsive romantic behavior because they create shame. In this way, we can understand compulsive sexual and romantic behavior as a desperate attempt to solve the unsolvable–sex and love addiction is a desperate solution to the cultural double bind.

The following illustrations of the four cultural beliefs include the many different lies women internalize about sexuality and love. As you read the stories, you might ask yourself which cultural lies you have inherited.

Cultural Belief Number One: I must be good to be worthy of love

Women with this belief may have grown up in strongly religious environments. They may have families who were from the "right" neighborhoods. They often come from families in which one or more of their caregivers were addicts.

Women who believe they must be "good" to earn love often become perfectionists. Perfectionism can manifest in many ways: overachieving in work or volunteer activities, taking on too many tasks in a church or home, spending inordinate amounts of time on personal appearance, or carrying high expectations of children, friends, or family.

Cultural Belief Number One is in direct conflict with Cultural Belief Number Three (If I am sexual, I am bad). So a woman who is compelled to be "good" may disown her sexuality. She does this because she believes sex is bad and, therefore, she cannot be sexual and still be worthy of love. Women with this belief are at risk for sexual anorexia. In this case, a woman shuts down sexually, either in a relationship or outside a relationship. A woman with this belief may attract partners with the following traits:

The partner who is beneath her and who she can be sexual with.
These partners often are not as ambitious as she is. They do not come from the same kinds of families or display traits that challenge her. They often like her more than she likes them. They will work to please her, meeting her expectations. She will be able to have sex with these partners initially because she will not find them threatening. However, over time, her sexual interest may fade. Frequently these partners are addicted to alcohol, drugs, or sex.

The partner who she feels less than, and who demands perfection.
These partners often display arrogance and grandiosity. They act as if they are a god, and demand saintly perfection from their female partners. They are self-righteous or controlling, thinking they know best. These partners make decisions

unilaterally and anger easily. If they do not get their way, they can be emotionally punitive or physically violent. They may become sexually abusive. At times, they also lose sexual interest in their partner. They may have secret affairs or a hidden relationship with pornography. Frequently they are addicted to their work.

Heather

You may remember Heather from other chapters. Heather sought therapy for the first time because her behavior had become compulsive. She found herself cutting off her romantic feelings for lovers even when she didn't want to. It scared her. She began to see how she might truly be unable to stay in a relationship with someone she was attracted to and cared for. Heather was raised to be a good girl and in her family, having sexual feelings was not part of being good.

Her reputation was important for her family who were visible people in their community. So Heather developed a fear of being sexual. She cut off this part of herself with all her other feelings. However, when she was a freshman in high school she found herself drawn to Mark, and for the next 10 years her feelings for him ruled her life. They were never officially a couple, but Heather devoted her emotional energy to thinking of him every day and planning for ways to be around him. After graduating from high school, Heather followed Mark out of state where he was attending college. She enrolled in the same university.

Although Heather was no longer under the watchful eye of her parents and their community, she was still concerned about being a good girl and protecting her reputation. Her sexual relationship with Mark was a secret. Mark had a girlfriend so he only called Heather when he was drunk and wanted sex. To hide her unmanageable feelings for Mark, which she now identifies as love addiction, Heather's sexual behavior escalated. She began having sex with many men as a way to avoid thinking of Mark. She chose men to have sex with that she didn't care for or barely knew. If a man wanted to get close to her, she dropped him. In therapy, Heather talked about her romantic life in brief spurts.

I only slept with guys I felt better than. I would meet one guy for breakfast, another for lunch, and another for dinner.

As a way to protect her reputation, her sexual encounters were with men who weren't in her social circles. Heather seduced and had sex with men her friends didn't know, men she met in restaurants, internships, libraries, or bars. She kept a list of how many men she slept with. The list included married men, friends' boyfriends, and the brothers of previous boyfriends. These guys were always men she felt were "beneath" her. Heather explains,

I knew I was gaining a feeling of power with this behavior, but it came with so much pain because deep down, I still yearned for Mark.

Years later in therapy, she wonders if the pain of her addiction to Mark created her sexually avoidant behavior.

I think deep down I told myself no one would ever have that kind of power over me again. So I never let anyone get close.

After college, Mark married. Heather finally gave up hope of being with him and moved to Los Angeles. She dated lots of men and tried to become intimate with them. But each time a relationship grew too close, Heather ended it. She always found a reason that made sense to her–she didn't like his family, his career choice, or she disapproved of his religious practice. Then she met Jake. Jake had it all: a promising career, a lovely home in the Hollywood hills, and he adored Heather. He spent lavish amounts of money on her, took her on trips, and seemed to enjoy everything about her. It was everything she thought she wanted in a man. But Heather could not sustain a connection with Jake. She ended the relationship with him one weekend after the two shared a romantic getaway. She had lost all desire for him. Again, she had cut off her feelings, but this time she didn't want to. Terribly afraid, confused and disturbed, she made an appointment with a therapist the next day.

Cultural Belief Number Two: I am not really a woman unless someone desires me sexually or romantically

When a woman's sense of self is broken, she's at risk for basing her identity on her desirability. When Cultural Belief Number Two becomes part of her belief system, she feels she must be sexy in order to be a woman. Often a woman with this belief will become romantic with someone because she was "chosen" rather than making a choice of her own. She may or may not find this person attractive. The person finds her irresistible and she gains ego strength from this dynamic. She borrows her functioning from feeling desired. It's about being wanted. She uses seduction to feel good and gain a sense of power. She may have many partners at the same time or one right after the other–using seduction to gain power over others–needing to be sexually desired to feel good about herself. Being wanted is the same thing as being alive.

Sex and the City contains many examples of Cultural Belief Number Two. The main character, Carrie, and her on-again, off-again boyfriend, Mr. Big, are a good example. In the initial stages of romance, the couple cleverly finds ways to seduce and flirt with one another. Although Carrie is clearly "falling in love" with Mr. Big, their relationship remains perpetually undefined. It leaves room for one or the other to have other lovers. At one point, Carrie is shocked when she finds Mr. Big at dinner with another woman. Instead of curtailing her attempts to keep Big interested, she turns to her obsession–buying shoes–and the relationship torments her through several seasons. Mr. Big says just enough to keep Carrie "hooked" without ever truly committing to her. She is caught in a cycle of perpetually seducing him with clever dialogue, sexy clothing, and regular sex.

In the same series, Samantha's character embodies the belief that "unless someone desires me sexually, I'm not really a woman." She seduces one man after another, thriving on the power that comes from knowing she is sexually attractive.

Cultural Belief Number Two is developmentally confining. Beneath a grown-up façade, a woman is frozen in her youth. Emotionally, she may be anywhere from five to seventeen years of age, and deep down, she may be angry with men. Her anger usually started at a young age when she first became aware of being sexually objectified in a way that made her feel powerless or ashamed. As a result, she will be drawn to partners who are emotionally immature. They will have the following characteristics:

- emotionally undeveloped and unavailable
- periodically act like children
- chronically underemployed or financially unstable
- set her up for care-taking
- illicit her sense of pity
- aggravate and annoy her at times
- abuse substances

Maria

After her divorce, Maria became involved with a man addicted to drugs and sex. She was irresistibly drawn to Jerry. She found him sexy, and also felt weak with his seduction techniques. He pursued her and made her feel like a woman. After the lack of sexual energy she experienced in her marriage, Maria was starved for this type of attention. But Jerry's addictions affected his life. He had difficulty keeping commitments, had trouble managing his finances, and seemed to always be tired. In fact, he couldn't seem to motivate himself to pursue much of anything. Over a few months time, Maria realized she was competing for attention with his use of drugs and other women. She always felt his emotional distance. She couldn't seem to reach him. But she stayed in the relationship because the sex was so intense. Jerry made her feel desired. She confronted his emotional distance but he always knew just what to say to keep Maria "hooked."

Over time, Maria grew angry and threatened by Jerry's involvement with other women. Like Heather, she compensated for her feelings by having sex with other men. She was addicted to Jerry, so she couldn't leave him. She just used other men to feel more powerful and secure. Jerry got suspicious of Maria's behavior (because it was similar to his own, he always seemed suspicious). One night after an argument on the telephone, Jerry snuck into her home. Rather than feel intruded upon or afraid, Maria felt desired. It wasn't until she shared this event with her 12-step group months later that she realized she was spinning out of control. Her sponsor helped her see Jerry's inappropriate boundary violation, and how Maria didn't realize that boundaries were OK to have. Although Maria was still sexual with Jerry on numerous occasions after he came into her home uninvited, her 12-step meetings and the support of her therapist ultimately helped her give up her "drug" of choice.

Maria then withdrew from dating and sex. During her withdrawal, she realized that fear and sexual arousal were fused for her. Since her household had been a dangerous place to be a child, and she had used fantasy and masturbation to cope, unconsciously, she was trying to reconcile this trauma. By dating Jerry and using sex to feel powerful and secure, she only kept her original trauma alive. Sadly, this left Maria either with partners she found sexually undesirable or ones who were emotionally unavailable and perhaps dangerous. As her time in recovery lengthened, Maria's fear of men diminished. Her self-development deepened and her behavior matured. She began to find it possible to be attracted to men who were her equal.

Brooklyn
Similar to Maria, Brooklyn's traumatic history fused fear and sexual desire. Her stepfather was a frightening man, and had sexualized Brooklyn in her prepubescent and adolescent years. As a woman, Brooklyn found herself playing out her original trauma by engaging in risky sexual activities that included trading sex for drugs. When she married, she chose a man addicted to cocaine. She moved Ray into her home and purchased a new car for him. She cooked his meals, did his laundry, and had sex with him any time he desired her. She was convinced she could change Ray and replace his use of drugs by being the perfect wife. What she didn't realize is that an addict already has a relationship. She was competing with her husband's first love–drugs.

When her efforts to get what she wanted from the relationship failed, she grew resentful. She returned to her former sexual behavior and took secret lovers. Although her husband knew nothing of her infidelity, the tension in their home grew and the fighting escalated. His drug use increased, and so did his rage. On one particular occasion, a verbal fight became violent. She dialed 911, but when the police arrived she sent them away. She was overcome with pity for her husband.

I felt sorry for him. I couldn't bear to see them take him away in the police car. I told my husband to hide in the back of the house, and I lied to the cops telling them I thought someone was trying to break into our home and that's why I called.

Although they separated shortly after this episode, Brooklyn still finds herself drawn to her husband and wants to reconcile. She has not yet accepted that she's addicted to her husband and to sexual intensity. She needs a great deal of support to intervene on her unhealthy patterns.

Cultural Belief Number Three: If I am sexual, I am bad
Cultural Belief Number Three is unavoidable in Western culture. It's a rare woman who can embrace her sexuality in healthy ways by avoiding the powerful

belief that her sexuality is bad. As a result of belief number three, a woman feels that if she wants to be sexual, something must be wrong with her. She has difficulty owning sexual desire. She must reject her sexual self or tolerate the idea that she's bad. This is a painful paradox and manifests in a few different ways:

- ► She can shut down sexually in order to escape the horrible feeling that comes with sexual activity. Her sexual anorexia is an attempt to escape the feeling that she's bad.

- ► She can find "bad" boys to be sexual with. Bad boys have no trouble being sexual. Their sexuality is overt. They are not really bad. They simply become the receptacle for the negative sex feelings she's inherited. In this kind of partnership, he initiates sex and she submits. Her partner's overt sexuality allows her disowned sexual desires to be released. Oftentimes after a sexual encounter she experiences feelings of rage. She's trying to distance from the bad feelings bubbling up from her sexual encounter. The feelings get projected on to her partner and she sees him as dirty or perverted. These negative sex thoughts are truly her intolerable feelings about herself. In an effort to avoid this unbearable reality, she projects it on to her partner.

- ► She may find herself only aroused when experiencing pain or humiliation. The degrading experience that accompanies her sexual encounter strengthens her belief that she's a bad person if she is sexual.

- ► She may only have sex when not fully alert. For example, she may use alcohol or other drugs to lower her awareness and block the shameful feelings that accompany sex. She may only have sex upon first waking or when almost asleep. She may only have sex after viewing provocative material that stimulates her and allows her to disconnect from her feelings.

- ► She may become addicted to seductive role sex (flirting and attracting potential lovers while disliking sex or being sexual with them).

- ► She may only orgasm during solitary masturbation that she keeps separate from her experience with a lover and from her own reality. If she were to admit to masturbating, it feels like an admission of being bad. Therefore, her sexual self is a secret. It has its own compartment. She keeps it separate.

- ► She may have sex with married men or have extramarital affairs as an expression of her secretive need to be sexual, and further compartmentalize her sexual self.

Amelia

Amelia, a thirty-five-year-old librarian, consulted a therapist after her husband told her he "couldn't stand being married to a fat woman" and asked for a divorce. Amelia had always struggled with her weight, but had gained more than ever during her marriage, carrying an extra 100 pounds. Married three years, Amelia's desire to be sexual with her husband ceased shortly after their wedding. At the same time, her desire for food increased.

Amelia was raised in a rigid fundamentalist family where she had been taught that sex was bad. As a result, she feared being seen as sexual. She had a sister who was promiscuous and she used to feel superior to her because she was not sexual. Her rejection of her sexuality had never been a problem for Amelia until she married. She assumed being married would make sex OK. But this did not happen, and Amelia turned to food to soothe and comfort herself. After the divorce Amelia lost weight. She was able to wear clothing that made her feel desirable. She began to like her body, and the attention she was getting from other men.

Her sexual feelings returned. To deal with them, she began to masturbate. Although she was discovering pleasure in her new sexual feelings, she also feared she might be like her sister. She didn't want to be seen as promiscuous, so her sexual behavior stayed secret. Eventually, she became lonely. She wanted to be with a partner. Although she was no longer overweight, she still felt like a "fat girl" inside. Amelia's insecurity about her body, as well as her deeply held belief that sex is bad, kept her hostage.

In an effort to meet her need for companionship, Amelia turned to an escort service. She used the inheritance from her parents that she had been saving for retirement to pay an escort for secret, romantic encounters. She hired an escort to take her to fancy restaurants and hotels. During these encounters, Amelia felt like a different person. She could have sex without anyone knowing. She began living a double life. In an effort to stay separate from her regular life, Amelia preferred to go out of town with her paid companions. She wore revealing clothing, made out in the limousine, and asked her escort to take her to places she had always wanted to go. After these "dates," as she called them, she sometimes struggled with feelings of shame. She could feel depressed for a few days only to find herself planning for the next weekend of sex in an effort to feel better.

Amelia's behavior continued and she became more desperate. It was as if her need for sex couldn't be satiated. No amount was enough. She started meeting men in bars, going to their homes to have sex. Sometimes she experimented with drugs, and discovered the lure of cocaine. She enjoyed the added high it brought to a sexual encounter. Amelia was losing ground to her compulsive habits. She was tired all the time and her work at the library began to suffer. She was terribly lonely. She was making hints to her therapist about what was going on, but her therapist was missing them. Amelia finally one day told her therapist everything she was doing and he referred her to a sex and love addiction specialist who would be better suited for her needs.

Amelia was quite shy on her first visit to her new therapist. But Glenda was warm with a gentle confidence about her. With some gentle questioning, Amelia was able discuss her behavior and felt some immediate relief with the honest sharing. Glenda was able to help Amelia name her behavior as sex and love addiction. Amelia was resistant to the concept and assured her therapist that she was not an addict and could stop the behavior herself.

Over time, however, she discovered that she couldn't. In fact, her acting out became worse. As she began to surrender to the reality of her problem, her therapist urged her to join a support group for other women addicted to sex and love. She resisted attending 12-step meetings for sex and love addicts, but began going to Overeaters Anonymous to treat her food issues.

For Amelia and many women, it's easier to address food issues than to explore sexuality. There is less cultural shame attached to food addiction than to sexual addiction. On her own, however, Amelia explored literature about sex and love addiction. She has discontinued her use of escorts and decreased her masturbation.

Without the high of sex, however, her food issues are more prevalent as she's turned again to food for comfort. Her weight has increased over the past month, and she is uncomfortable with her body. She's made an addictive switch, which is a prevalent pattern for women around food and sex. In time, as her food issues stabilize, she will be able to address her sexual addiction more fully.

Cultural Belief Number Four: I must be sexual to be loveable

Women with this belief feel their worth is determined by how many people want them sexually. They feel they must be sexual to have love. They need a great deal of approval and acceptance, and look to a lover to provide a sense of worth. They may dress provocatively, creating an image and a body to catch a partner. Women with this belief are in a perfect position to attract a sex-addicted partner because they confuse sex with love. Carnes calls these women sexual "co-addicts."

Carnes' insight into the partner of a sex addict is helpful and congruent with what we find with Cultural Belief Number Four. Women who feel this way are in reaction to this belief whether they have a partner or not. This is a direct result of the cultural sexual objectification of women.

Cultural Belief Number Four teaches women how to live to please others. They live as commodities: as objects to serve, to be consumed, or to be desired. It's an incredibly painful way to live. Women come to the point of despair at different times in life.

For Jane, the pain of living to please became unmanageable in her early thirties. She consulted a therapist when her empty sexual life became too painful. Jane felt her most attractive feature was to attract and please men. In therapy, she articulated that the felt compelled to please them:

When I am with a man, I become a different woman. I am giggly, flirty, and it's no wonder no one takes me seriously. It's automatic. It's like he has power over me instantly, even without trying.

Eventually Jane became so disillusioned by her experiences with men that she gave up on relationships and began prostituting. She felt most useful during a sexual encounter where she received money. In therapy, she discussed a deeply held belief that while she was preparing for a sexual encounter, performing for a man, and receiving payment, her father would be proud of her.

I think I have been trained for this. It's effortless. It's easy, and yet I can't believe I am doing it. I'm two-selves. The one who has always been pleasing men since I can remember, and the one who also is a feminist and who knows this is crazy. I feel insane.

Conflicting Cultural Beliefs

The toxic combination of family trauma and negative cultural beliefs create great pain for women. Rarely does a woman internalize only one or two of these beliefs. It's more common that all four lies interact to form her belief about sex, about being a woman, and about love. Because these beliefs are in conflict with one another, they present a double bind. Women are caught in a terrible impasse that sets up fertile ground for sex and love to become addictive. Addiction perverts sex and love further, adding a dimension of greed. One woman described it this way:

I want more. Even after a sexual encounter, I feel myself yearning, longing, wishing for more. It's never enough. Sometimes, I think I am an endless well of need. My definition of addiction is simply more.

Chapter Six
The Body Knows

Pain is patterned and stored physically and chemically in our nervous, immune, and endocrine systems; it is in the bodymind.
Dr. Christiane Northrup, *Women's Bodies, Women's Wisdom*[1]

Exploring sex and love addiction means encountering your trauma. You may already be aware of the family and cultural abuse you have endured that has brought you to this exploration of addictive relationships. For many women, however, this isn't the case. They enter treatment with little or no memory of childhood trauma. For a therapist who's trained to treat sex and love addiction, a woman's lack of memory is suspect. Professionals treating this disease have a keen awareness of post-traumatic stress disorder, which alters brain chemistry and provides an environment fertile for addictions.

Absence of memory can be an indicator of PTSD. In some cases, survivors may have complete or partial amnesia regarding their traumatic histories. Trauma can damage the memory center in the brain, leaving memory distorted, fragmented or completely absent. Cortisol, a hormone released in the body during intense stress, plays a significant role in memory loss. Research shows that the hippocampus, our memory center, is sensitive to cortisol. High levels of cortisol poisons hippocampal cells and, over time, cause the hippocampus to shrink. Therefore, a lack of memory can indicate unhealthy levels of stress and trauma during formative years.[2]

If a child is unduly stressed, cortisol floods her body to reduce the amount of adrenaline and norepinephrine in her system. Cortisol brings the body back into homeostasis. It serves an important purpose. But it's toxic to the memory. If a child has loving adults to help her make sense of abusive, chaotic, or tragic events, her body needs less cortisol. The comfort of safe relationships determines whether a traumatic event will lead to long-term damage that results in PTSD.

We know that psychological isolation alters the brain. Impaired memory function is one way the brain is altered. This is a lovely design–a lack of memory is a protective device to help humans survive extreme situations without becoming immobilized with fear and pain. However, for an adult exploring her addiction, lack of memory can be very frustrating. It can add to her sense of shame and brokenness. There's nothing she can tie her behavior to. She cannot see the pain and shame that rests underneath her need for addictive escape. For this reason, we have found that a critical part of recovery and treatment for sex and love addiction is an understanding of brain chemistry and how it works. Additionally, it's imperative to respect the many ways our bodies store and respond to trauma.

The Body Talks

Patterns of addictive sexual and romantic behavior parallel traumatic history. It's as if each woman has an internal map for the way her sex and love addiction will unfold. Her internal map, or trauma history, dictates the way she will behave addictively. She doesn't need to be aware of the map for it to direct her behavior. The memory center in her brain may not recall the details of her traumatic past, but her body does. Her body stores the memories. Her body has its own wisdom, and it tells her story through actions, illness, and emotions. In the words of Northrup, "Unresolved traumatic events from the past live in the energy system of the body..."[3]

A woman may experience reactions to sexuality and touch that are beyond her conscious choice. These automatic reactions are telling the story of her trauma and may include some of the following:

- fear of sex
- lack of sexual desire or interest
- intrusive and unpleasant sexual thoughts
- panicky feelings when touched or emotional distance during sex
- nausea during sex
- unhealthy sexual desires and interests that cause problems in relationships
- touch means sex
- seeing an erection or a partner's sexual arousal means you have a job to do
- automatically surveying a new environment for sexual opportunities
- feeling like you have two distinct personalities
- finding partners who are emotionally unavailable

Addictive Relationships

Trauma survivors do not separate the addictive need for escape from the addictive need for love. The two are merged. As a result, relationships that start out intense, passionate, or chaotic may feel like true love. For women with normal neurochemistry, these types of relationships indicate danger or probable heartache.

But for a survivor, the adrenaline that comes with addictive relationships feels normal. She's accustomed to feeling out of balance, scared, or on alert. In fact, most survivors are on constant red alert. Trauma survivors are highly tuned into their environments because as children they had to be. Typically, they have an "all or nothing" response to emotional stimuli. They are prone to freeze or panic if they are confronted with criticism, anger, or perceived threat.

Sadly for adult survivors, intimacy is a threat. Close relationships have proven to be dangerous, unpredictable or suffocating. For these reasons, if a woman carries a great deal of unhealed wounding, she's not truly available for emotional intimacy, and her relationships will be difficult and painful. Anne Wilson Shaef calls these relationships "pseudo-relationships."[4] We call them addictive relationships.

In addictive relationships, the connection is hijacked from the start. It's a double bind to crave both connection and escape at the same time. There is a painful paradox in every addictive relationship–the paradox that in our deep desire to make connection, we keep large parts of ourselves out of connection. As a result, functional vulnerability is not present. Instead, a woman finds herself too vulnerable (needy, dependent, and afraid) or walled off (powerful, avoidant, and distrustful).

Addictive relationships give a woman a false sense of connection. They hide her fear of intimacy. She's often unaware of how lonely or afraid she is deep in her soul. While fearing intimacy and connection, she pursues a relationship and longs for closeness. She uses the relationship to provide her with the feelings she needs to function. Essentially, she borrows a sense of self and wholeness from the relationship. She uses the addictive relationship to satisfy her unmet needs, hide her fears, and escape her feelings of insecurity. This is not a true bond. This is an addictive bond.

When a woman has endured the trauma of psychological isolation in early development, her strategies of escape become compulsive and she uses them automatically. She will find herself baffled and confused. Why do relationships bring repeated failure and pain? Is it always her partner's fault, or is there a deeper problem? If you're exploring similar relationship pain, you may encounter the following realities:

▶ Your style of being in a relationship has become addictive.
▶ Addictive relationships are spiritually and emotionally empty.
▶ Addictive relationship patterns are abusive to yourself and your partner.

Heather

Heather's relationship with Mark was addictive. She experienced such intense feelings for him that she thought it was love. Since feelings were not tolerated in her family of origin, Heather had learned to depress her normal emotions in an attempt to adapt.

As a result, many of Heather's emotions were unrecognizable to her. She was a stranger to herself. So when she began the relationship with Mark, she had no ability to express feelings or needs.

In many ways, Heather was numb, which left her vulnerable to an intense, addictive experience that might jumpstart her feelings. She found this with Mark. Their relationship contained roller-coaster-like patterns of highs and lows. Although the feelings included betrayal, distrust, and passionate sex, the intensity of the relationship was a drink of fresh water for Heather. The "experience" became absorbing and addictive, but created terrible pain for her.

Remember, Mark had little interest in committing to Heather, and their relationship was a small part of his life. For Heather, the relationship was everything. Mark was her world. She settled for whatever Mark would give her. Although she felt miserable, she was addicted to the intensity in the relationship and confused it with love. Mark continued to have relationships with other women while Heather hung onto the illusion of intimacy.

Like Heather, many women find themselves mistaking intensity for intimacy. It's easy to confuse the two as our culture supports the illusion that intense relationships are intimate relationships. Addictive relationships, which are intense, may indeed appear to be deep and intimate on the outside. But inside the addictive relationship, two people remain disconnected, adversarial, and alone. In truth, addictive relationships are spiritually and emotionally bankrupt.

Signs of an addictive relationship

- The relationship breeds chronic shame.
- The relationship may be secretive or exploitive, using fear to generate intensity.
- The relationship may require you to be perfect.
- The relationship is not mutual; power is misused.
- The relationship violates your value system in some fashion.
- The relationship is passionate at first, but over time will become lifeless and the couple will grow increasingly isolated.
- The relationship doesn't permit self-care and time for individual pursuits or hobbies.
- The relationship may become dangerous.
- The relationship feels like part of a double life. You are a different person with your partner than with others in a way that doesn't feel comfortable.
- The relationship is based largely on fantasy not reality.

Addictive Relationships as Self-Abuse

Addictive relationships are self-abusive because they are about deprivation. A common phrase I hear from patients is, "I felt lonely after we made love, and found myself sorry that I tried to connect with him." While some forms of deprivation are more overt than others, deprivation is a unifying factor in each addictive relationship.

In an addictive relationship, a woman's need for nurturing, safety, and connection goes unmet. Although the relationship may include passionate sex or intense highs, it's the nutritional equivalent of chocolate cake or cotton candy at mealtime. It's like drinking a Coke when you're dehydrated on a hot day–if you are trying to quench your thirst, it doesn't happen. You just want more and more.

You may enjoy the initial sweetness, but will be left unsatisfied and thirstier than before. Similarly with an addictive relationship, it's never satisfying, never fulfilling, and it will leave you craving more. You'll find yourself thirsty for love and starved for authentic human connection. Like sugar, sex and love are addictive, and a woman can endure malnourishment for quite some time. Some addictive relationships go on for years.

Early in an addictive relationship there is a high. A woman feels more *self-confident,* mistaking grandiosity for inner strength. She may have an increased desire for action. Her actions, however, don't contain purpose, dignity, or value. They bring harm to her and to others. Over time the addictive relationship lets her down. It becomes all-powerful and all-consuming, yet the initial high can no longer compete with the shame and despair.

Addictive relationships deprive a woman of the joy that comes with being known and knowing another person intimately. Chronic deprivation solidifies her belief that she is unworthy of love. The more deprived she becomes, the more fuel she has for compulsive behavior. If the relationship is long term, the chronic deprivation further hollows out the neural pathways that her original trauma started, and alters her dopamine and serotonin levels. Her trauma symptoms progressively grow worse.

Sexual Anorexia

For some sex and love addicts, isolation becomes a refuge. One client summed it up this way, "I don't know how not to be lonely." It's important to distinguish between solitude and isolation. Solitude is a nourishing experience that allows a woman time to connect with herself and enables her to be present for her life. Isolation is not the same. Isolation is deprivation in the extreme and comes from a terror of human connection.

The need for intimacy brings such intense fear that it's easier to avoid it completely. Isolation involves shutting out other people in an attempt to hide. The long-term effects of isolation keep negative core beliefs alive. Being isolated feels safe because it takes extreme energy to be with others while keeping parts of the self compartmentalized. When someone chooses to isolate, it's an attempt to take off the mask. The mask is the face used to please others, giving them the illusion that all is OK.

To understand sexual anorexia, one must understand the devastating impact of trauma that would cause a woman to prefer isolation to human connection. Research shows us that when trauma happens at the hands of trusted family members, it's more difficult to integrate and heal than trauma that happens in nature, with a stranger, or during an accident. When children suffer in their own families, their need for connection and human contact is devastated. This need becomes something to be feared. Recognition of needing someone must be rejected in order for the child to feel safe. Needing someone increases a child's vulnerability, and if the caregivers are physically, emotionally, or sexually abusive, needs represent danger. Children rely on adults for food and touch. When the adults have proven not to be trustworthy, the child will learn to hate these particular needs. It's a tragic response to trauma.

Sexual anorexia is rejection of human connection at the most core level. When a woman becomes sexually anorexic, she suppresses her desire for sexual and emotional contact in an effort to preserve her isolation, which is her illusion of safety. You may remember Maggie from earlier chapters. As a young girl, she found refuge in her room reading books. Her family life taught her that connection and relationships weren't safe. Isolation became her best friend, her trusted partner, her only refuge. In this way, sexual anorexia, like addiction, becomes the relationship. It becomes addictive. A woman attaches to being alone much like someone attaches to a substance to feel better and safe.

To better understand sexual anorexia, it's helpful to compare it to food anorexia. Sex, like food, is meant to be sustaining and nourishing. Eating and making love are also designed for pleasure. For women, food and sex represent something taken into the body. Penetration is involved with both eating and sexual intercourse. For abuse survivors, penetration is a complicated issue. It often represents violation, so in an effort to feel safe, a woman learns to control what goes into her mouth and into her vagina.

When a woman starves herself, it's less about the food than the need for food. There is a complete hatred for hunger because hunger represents a need. Josie, a client who struggled with both sexual anorexia and food anorexia, remembers jogging through town one evening, feeling hungry, but determined to avoid food. She remembers looking into the restaurant windows as she passed by on the sidewalks.

I felt rage toward the people inside, happily eating. How could they be enjoying food when I had to be out here running and depriving? Why couldn't I be like them? And at the same time, I felt they were disgusting. I wanted to hurt them, so I stared into the windows as I passed by and scowled at them, feeling disdain and hoping they would feel ashamed of themselves for indulging.

Josie's rage toward others who were enjoying food and life is typical of the anorexic. The anorexic strives to shut off all recognition of her appetite in an attempt to control her needs and, therefore, her world. Her rigorous control forces her into deprivation.

Like the food anorexic, the sexual anorexic is terrified of her need. She starves herself from the experience of sexuality. She exerts control over her sexual appetite by shutting it down completely, maintaining a sense of control over her body. Any recognition of sexual desire is detested, both in herself and others. Women caught in the addictive cycle of sexual anorexia live in a constant state of deprivation, and when confronted with sexuality, anorexics can become stern, judgmental, or self-righteous.

In Chapter Five, we discussed sex as core to the self. When sex is shut down or avoided, the whole self is shut down and rejected. Sexual anorexia causes extreme emotional, sexual, spiritual deprivation because it is a total abhorrence of the self. There is an irony to sexual anorexia that is noteworthy. In their attempt to avoid sex, women who are sexually anorexic are preoccupied with sexuality. Their efforts to avoid sex have a hypervigilant quality that is all-consuming and repetitive. Carnes developed the following list as helpful indicators for sexual anorexia:[5]

- a dread of sexual pleasure
- a morbid and persistent fear of sexual contact
- obsession and hypervigilance around sexual matters
- avoidance of anything connected with sex
- preoccupation with others being sexual
- distortions of body appearance
- extreme loathing of body functions
- obsessional self-doubt about sexual adequacy
- rigid, judgmental attitudes about sexual behavior
- excessive fear and preoccupation with sexually transmitted diseases
- obsessive concern or worry about the sexual intentions of others
- shame and self-loathing over sexual experiences
- depression about sexual adequacy and functioning
- intimacy avoidance because of sexual fear
- self-destructive behavior to limit, stop, or avoid sex

A sexually anorexic woman is similar to a sexually addicted woman. Both obsess about sex. Both avoid intimacy. Both live in a constant state of deprivation because they suffer the absence of authentic connection that comes with healthy intimacy. Emotional deprivation is the core of sexual anorexia and sexual addiction. In fact, the root of both is a hatred of the need for human closeness and connection. Closeness means disappointment, abandonment, and pain. Connection brings terror. Sexual anorexia is an extreme aversion to closeness, and sexual addiction is an objectification of the other person that makes closeness impossible. Both extremes lead to isolation and profound self-abuse.

Sexual anorexia: aversion
Maggie's story is one of extreme relational avoidance in conjunction with food deprivation. Her growing despair about the lack of intimacy in her life represents the pain of the disease. She feels powerless to experience love and connection. Over time, Maggie is finding it more difficult to be part of social activities with her friends, and she's disillusioned with her work. Her sexual and emotional deprivation touches every aspect of her life.

Sexual anorexia: binge/purge patterns
According to Carnes, sexual anorexics are also:

... prone to sexual bingeing-occasional periods of extreme sexual promiscuity, or "acting out" in much the way that bulimics will binge with compulsive overeating and then purge by self-induced vomiting.[6]

The foundation of Barbara's sexual addiction is this type of sexual anorexia. While Barbara didn't have many friends or romantic opportunities growing up, she did marry–three times. In her first two marriages, she experienced a profound lack of intimacy. Barbara's story illustrates the relationship between food, sexual addiction, and sexual anorexia. The eating disorder and the compulsive sexual behavior serve to medicate feelings of pain and loneliness. They cover the pain of codependency. When she was thin, she felt sexual. When she was in a committed relationship, she gained weight and struggled with sexual intimacy with her partner. Her sexual behavior was impulsive and fast. Like bulimia, she took in sexual partners quickly without knowing them. Later, when she felt badly, she discarded them. She was unable to bond to anyone.

In this way, her sexual disorder kept her hungry. She didn't strictly avoid sex or relationships, but like a bulimic, she couldn't take in the nourishment of human connection. The pattern continued as a way to keep Barbara from facing how vulnerable and dependent she truly was. Both addictions covered up the painful reality of her original family trauma. They also served to hide her profound fear of intimacy. Barbara's addictions kept her negative self-image alive and put her life in danger.

Addictive Relationships as Abuse of Power

Like sexual anorexia, addictive relationships lead to isolation and profound deprivation. In this way, addictive relationships also become self-abusive. But addictive relationships involve a partner. They are abusive to others. In addictive relationships, there is a constant struggle for power–who has it and who doesn't. Some couples wrestle with who works harder, who's more organized, who's a better parent, or perhaps who is more sexual. Sexual struggles are about power, and the person who has the least desire for sex holds the power.

In healthy couples, there is an awareness of power and a respect for how it is handled. Both partners genuinely wish to see the other thrive, and work to maintain a balance of power in the relationship. If one person is making a change that increases his/her power, the relationship adapts to hold the change. And although both partners may endure discomfort during the change, they work together to re-balance the dynamic when possible, knowing that mutuality is the key to intimacy and connection.

One way that power becomes imbalanced in a relationship is with secrets. Addictive relationships thrive on secrets. Secrets are about power and control. When you have a secret, you present a distorted picture of who you really are. You make the choice to withhold information that might affect your partner's desire to be with you. In this way, you exert control over the relationship. For victims of abuse, the need to be in control is a natural response to trauma.

However, this kind of control in a relationship can destroy the chance for intimacy.

There are different kinds of secrets. Some secrets are more overt than others and initially create more problems when they are revealed. For example, a secret affair can be more damaging to a couple than a secret feeling of anger that didn't get expressed in a timely manner. It's important to understand, however, hidden feelings become corrosive over time. When emotions are chronically hidden or secretive, they unravel the fabric of a relationship. Not only are both individuals robbed of the richness that comes from knowing each other, but the energy it takes to withhold the truth eventually kills sexual desire.

Overt Secrets

Overt secrets are the lies we tell ourselves and others. They range from culturally supported little white lies to larger, more deceptive untruths. Secrets are a way to maintain an illusion of power and control. Secrets allow you to control someone's impression of you, hide your true self, and maintain a false sense of security. You may find yourself lying automatically and compulsively. Here are a few examples:

Hidden Spending. Spending money that is not within the limits of your family/household, keeping a secret bank account, paying for items that are outside your value system (sex, drugs, and/or gambling).

Sexual Acting Out. Having sex outside the rules of the relationship you are in, whether it's hiding Internet use, pornography use, other lovers, masturbation, emotional affairs, and flirtations.

Boundary Violations. Looking through a partner's personal belongings, i.e. cell phone calls, files, e-mails, and clothing; stalking or following a love interest, and listening in on phone conversations.

Disordered Eating. The binge/purge cycle can be hidden from a partner/family member. The food obsession takes energy and focus. The obsession doesn't allow room for intimacy with others.

Other Addictions. Lying about alcohol use and drug use. Addicts may hide their substance abuse in an attempt to conceal the truth from family members or partners.

Covert Secrets

Covert secrets are unconscious beliefs, impaired ways of thinking, and hidden emotions that direct your behavior. They are often largely unconscious. The work of therapy is to uncover these secrets so that you can better know yourself, and understand your intentions and actions. Without an understanding of your covert secrets, you remain a stranger to yourself and to your partner. Your body knows your secrets even if your brain doesn't.

This is how you can act angry without knowing you're angry. Without an understanding of your covert secrets, you cannot truly share who you are, and your relationships will eventually grow tired and stale. In fact, covert secrets can lead to sexual anorexia.

Core Cultural Beliefs (refer to Chapter Two): Core beliefs include the feeling that you are unworthy, defective, and will always be alone. They include internalized sexism, homophobia, and misogynism. Self-hate grows from these core beliefs.

Grief: Our culture doesn't allow time for grief. Grief is a messy process. When we grieve, we cannot function at full capacity. In a consumer culture that needs people to be fast, productive and "on," it makes sense that many women have not had time to grieve the losses in their lives–loss of children, loved ones, lovers, pets, and dreams.

Shame: Shame is the unbearable sense that "I'm not OK." Shame can be the result of a woman's own behavior and it can also be carried shame. Carried shame happens when someone acts in a shameful manner toward you and they don't take responsibility for their actions. As a result, you wear the shame that the perpetrator should be wearing. We see this in the case of a rape victim or incest survivor. Both feel the shame of the offender. Both feel it was somehow their fault. Remember, shame drives addictive behavior, so victims of sexual abuse are vulnerable to addiction.

Anger: In our culture, if a woman is angry, she gets labeled in various negative ways–bitch, control freak, irrational, or hysterical. Often times, she's shamed for her anger with damaging words that are sexual in nature. For these reasons and others, women find it very difficult to identify and express anger. Hidden or repressed anger will find a way out. It can't stay buried. Anger can become eroticized. It may be sexually expressed as anorexia, infidelity, or aggressive sexual behavior.

Anger

For the healthiest relationships, anger is a difficult emotion to handle. For women, anger can be the trigger point for sex becoming an addiction. Remember Maria's story. She tried to cope with Jerry's drug and sex addiction by seeking out other men. Her anger took her into sexual acting out that was dangerous and risky. Her thinking was something like this: "If you can flirt with other women, I will show you...I'll find other men and see how you like it!" Her sexual addiction was a way to cope with her love addiction to Jerry.

Stephen Karpman, a transactional psychologist, has provided the field of psychology a model to understand how anger plays out in relationships. The Karpman triangle illustrates the dramatic roles individuals play in daily life when they are dealing with anger.[7] There are three roles: victim, persecutor, and rescuer.

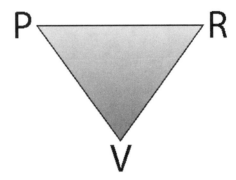

Victim: the person who appears submissive, or one down

Persecutor: the person who pressures or persuades the victim who may appear one up

Rescuer: the one who decides to intervene and help the situation (not a separate person necessarily).

Each role is ultimately unsatisfactory, repetitive, and generates misery for both people. It's called a triangle because each person takes turns playing the different roles in the system.

In the drama of anger, each person takes turns playing these roles. It's critical to understand that no one can stand being in the victim role for long. Victims will find a way to endure feeling one down by going one up. They may do this overtly by becoming the persecutor, or covertly by passively finding a way to express their anger, such as withholding secrets or sex.

In Maria's case, she couldn't bear feeling less than Jerry. Her attempt to overcome the victim role put her in the role of persecutor. She began keeping sexual secrets from Jerry. After a persecutor has been successful getting what she/he wants, she/he often moves into the role of rescuer to make the victim feel better. Maria would feel guilty after having sex with someone else, and in an attempt to feel better, she would spend lavish amounts of time and energy making Jerry happy and having sex with him. In this way, he had no idea what she was doing when he was not around. He became the victim.

Brooklyn
Remember from earlier chapters how Brooklyn first met her husband when he

was in rehab. He had no job or reliable source of income. Brooklyn had both. She moved him into her home and provided him with transportation. In essence, she rescued him. Brooklyn was in the position of providing. This is a power position. Receiving puts one in a position of vulnerability. The giver holds the power.

Soon into their marriage, Brooklyn became dissatisfied with their emotional and sex life. She began having an affair. Although the affair was a secret, the tension grew in their home. At one point during a fight, Ray physically threatened her. He became the persecutor. She became the victim. In truth, Brooklyn was also the persecutor because she had a powerful secret. And her husband was also a victim because he had a lack of information. Brooklyn called the police, but sent them away because she felt sorry for her husband. She became the rescuer.

The next day, Ray apologized repeatedly out of remorse and catered to her. He became the rescuer. This put Brooklyn once again in the one-up position, holding the power–and still holding a secret.

Brooklyn's relationship with Ray illustrates how each partner has an opportunity to play all three roles in the drama of anger. In an addictive relationship, the cycle of victim, persecutor, and rescuer repeats over and over, and without intervention, the drama gets worse. The hidden agendas and manipulation efforts gain strength and become dangerous and dark. The couple is left with the following choices: terminate the relation, get help, or surrender to a life of drama and chaos.

One client shared in therapy how she persecuted her husband in an effort to deal with her feelings of being a victim.

I baked his favorite cakes and desserts because I knew he couldn't resist. I loved watching him lose control over his appetite. It gave me such a feeling of power to see him get fat, and deep down, I knew this was unhealthy for him. I think I wanted him to die.

While her husband may have considered the food her expression of love and nurturing, her intent was just the opposite. Her anger, although covert, was destructive and cruel.

Erotic Rage

An entire book could be devoted to this topic. Anger merged with sexuality takes many forms and is prevalent in our culture. If you're struggling with sex and love addiction, you will encounter your rage as you become aware of the motivations behind your compulsive romantic and sexual behavior. Rage is the combination of shame and anger. It can be silent or loud. Rage doesn't have to be screaming, throwing things or slamming doors, although it may be all of these things. Rage can be a silent brewing, a quiet seething that permeates your mind and soul. Rage is like poison. It hurts you and it hurts others.

As a woman, you know what it is to be hurt by others' rage. You live in a culture that doesn't like you. Sexism is alive and well, and even with great strides since the woman's movement, gender inequality still exists. It's impossible to live as a woman in America and not breathe in the anger directed at you. You see it on billboards, on television, and in cinema. You may feel it at work, in politics, and in your communities.

The statistics for rape in our culture are astounding. According to the National Center for Victims of Crime, a woman is sexually assaulted every 2½ minutes.[8] Incest has been cited as the most common form of child abuse in America. Exact numbers of incest victims vary due to the fact that incest remains an extremely under-reported crime. However, one of the leading researchers on child sexual abuse, David Finkelhor, estimates that 1 million Americans are victims of father-daughter incest, with 16,000 new cases occurring annually.[9]

What are some of the ways women act out rage erotically? If you are reading this chapter, you may already be aware of the power you have with your sexuality. It is one of the most accessible powers available to you. As a survivor, you have been a victim of misused power, and have not been taught healthy ways of expressing your power. As a result, you may use sexuality to gain power or give away your power in a relationship.

- You may feel that individuals have no responsibility to each other during sexual encounters.
- You may think sex is a commodity to either give or get.
- You may feel sex is about a man's needs instead of yours.
- You may think sex creates abuse and one person will always be hurt.
- You may feel sex is a duty you must perform, and find ways to escape this duty.
- You may rely on abusive pornography or fantasies to feel aroused.
- You may act out sexually in ways that hurt you by choosing partners who are involved with other people.
- You may hurt your partner by acting out sexually with other people.
- You may have sex when you don't really want to or find it impossible to say no to sexual contact that's offered to you.
- You may take sex from your partner even when he or she seems unwilling or uninterested.

Erotic rage is an indication that all is not well. Perhaps you are in a relationship that is unhealthy, or you have unresolved trauma issues that need healing. You could be acting out anger with your current lover that is meant for your original caregiver(s). Or you may withhold sex because you're angry with your partner for secretly watching pornography to masturbate. When your sexuality becomes a vehicle for expressing anger, sex is no longer a healthy expression of love. Over time, the ability to identify when you're angry may be lost. You don't feel anger, you feel the need for sex. Or instead of rage, you feel needy and dependent.

For a sex and love addict, much of the addiction is about rage. Anger and shame fuel the need to compulsively act out or act in. Sexual rage comes in many forms, including abusing others and abusing yourself. Some women abuse others by having intrusive sex, taking sex from someone vulnerable, or lying about their sexual behavior.

Maria and Brooklyn both channeled their angry feelings sexually. Barbara's sexual acting out, motivated by anger toward her husbands or her father, had a desperate, lonely quality that left her feeling sick. Women abuse themselves with erotic rage. By having a stream of anonymous partners, putting themselves at risk for disease and abuse, erotic anger becomes a way to hurt oneself.

Josie, a beautiful young woman in her early twenties, abused herself by maintaining an affair with a married man. She kept herself in a constant state of yearning and grief with this relationship. While her lover carried on his life with his wife and children, he seduced her with false hopes and promises. In this relationship, Josie endured regular yeast infections, an STD, an unwanted pregnancy, and regular humiliation. Her deprivation continued as she stayed with him, year after year. Josie couldn't acknowledge the anger she felt toward her lover. As a result, she acted it out on her own body.

Sexual Offending

Sexual aggression is about rage. As a victim of rape or incest, a woman carries this rage in her body and, eventually, it comes out erotically charged toward other people. Some women hurt men and children. We like to think this doesn't happen. It's difficult to discuss women as victims and in the same breath understand women as offenders.

But with an understanding of the Karpman triangle, we know that a victim will not stay powerless indefinitely. She'll find a way to use power to regain a sense of control after being victimized. In this way, some victims of sexual violence become perpetrators. Typically, if a woman is offending, she will not stop until there is some form of outside intervention, such as a terrible accident, police involvement, or loss of a child.

Sarah

Sarah is thirty-one-year-old professor at a local junior college, and is married with one young child. Sarah has been in treatment for an eating disorder for the past six years. In treatment, she has learned a great deal about her background, and how her eating disorder started. She was raised in a fundamentalist Christian home, and although her early years were filled with pleasant memories, everything abruptly changed when her mother died when she was nine. Sarah was left alone much of the time.

As minister of the church, her father was often busy and unavailable. Sarah gravely missed her mother. She felt lonely, sad, and forced to be a grown up. Sarah's father had no idea how to assist her and the church became his life. It was as if Sarah had lost two parents.

Sarah discovered that food made her feel better. She loved the feeling of being full. She remembers eating ice cream before bed each night. As she transitioned into adolescence, food was her best friend. She also turned to church activities for support and nurturing. She became involved in her youth group and spent most of her free time there. Tragically, at age twelve, Sarah was molested by her youth leader. He took advantage of his position, and Sarah's vulnerability and trust.

When Sarah's son approached the age of nine, the same age Sarah was at the time of her mother's death, she experienced a sudden weight gain and periods of intense rage and crying. After a year of therapy, Sarah trusted her counselor enough to reveal her deepest shame: she was having an affair with one of her students. Sarah was deeply troubled about lying to her husband. She felt ashamed of herself as a wife and mother. She was finding it difficult to complete lesson plans, grade papers, and be a mother. All she wanted to do was be with her lover. When the therapist confronted her about the power differential between herself and the student, Sarah didn't see a conflict because her lover was nineteen. The therapist was concerned about Sarah's lack of awareness, and took this as an opportunity to explore more deeply into Sarah's own abuse history.

In session, Sarah's therapist focused on Sarah's sexual history. Sarah revealed that she had found her father's pornography collection in the house while growing up. She liked the pictures of women, but felt that her body would never look as pretty. Sarah's father frequently made inappropriate comments about her body and how she was dressed. On one occasion, she remembers him saying, "You look fat in those pants. Take them off." She also heard her father's sexual comments about women in their church. She wondered why her father spent so much time with these women behind closed doors, and what she needed to do to get her father's attention.

As Sarah explored her sexual past, she identified a great deal of shame around her father's behavior. When Sarah was thirteen, her father was discovered receiving oral sex from one of the women in the church. As a result, he was "counseled" by church elders and sent to another church out of town. Sarah remembers this as a dark time in her life. She can't recall details of the move, her new home, or her new school. She had trouble making friends, and poured herself into her studies in an effort to survive.

Now, as an adult, Sarah is repeating her traumatic past. By having sex with her student, she is acting like her father and the youth leader who abused her. Both men abused their positions in the church, using them to gain sexual access to women and children. Sarah is using her power as an instructor similarly. Sarah's sexual behavior includes an intrusive element. Intrusive sex involves using a power position (clergy, teacher, therapist, employer) to be sexual with another person.

When Sarah realized the enormity of what she was doing with sex she felt overwhelmed and depressed. She felt dismay at the prospect of facing another addiction. The therapist reassured her that it seemed overwhelming to her now because it was new, and that she needed to proceed with small steps. Sarah's first step was to find a 12-step group for sex and love addicts. Further, she needed to realize that she could be sued for harassment, so her therapist recommended that she consult an attorney to explore her legal standing.

In therapy, Sarah also began to learn about the family of origin issues that led to her food addiction, and the newly discovered sex and love addiction. Losing her mother just prior to puberty was a horrible trauma. She had no one to turn to for comfort or questions about normal developmental issues young women face. Equally devastating was the spiritual abuse she experienced at the hands of her father and her youth leader. Both were "men of God" who abused their power sexually. As a result, Sarah learned to trust no one. Her spirituality and her sexuality had been terribly damaged.

After many therapy sessions and 12-step meetings, Sarah began to understand why she was a sex and love addict. The eating disorder was just the tip of the iceberg. Sarah saw her sex and love addiction as her primary addiction. She became depressed as she realized how her childhood abandonment had profoundly affected her life. The depression grew so severe that Sarah and her therapist decided it was time for in-patient treatment. Sarah attended a facility that professionally and expertly handled the interaction between sexual addiction and food addiction. After a month of intensive in-patient treatment, Sarah began feeling new hope and focus. She poured herself into mothering and explored a new career as a landscape designer. As her recovery gained momentum, Sarah experienced her first real days of peace and authentic joy.

Addictive Relationships as Borrowed Functioning
Trauma Bonds

Susan just completed graduate school and has an MS in social work. She's seeing a therapist because she's in a destructive relationship that she cannot get out of. She has tried to break up with him numerous times, but always returns. He's an alcoholic but manages to make a living as an artist. He's successful around town, and she enjoys accompanying him to his art shows. Occasionally when they argue, he becomes violent. Recently, she had an abortion. She didn't feel safe enough to have a baby with him. She's acting outside her value system, yet she can't get away, and she doesn't know why.

Remember Susan from Chapter One? She can't escape her damaging relationship. She is in a trauma bond. A trauma bond is when a woman's terror of being alone is fused with a terrible need for negative intensity in her relationships. Being alone creates incredible anxiety for some sex and love addicts, putting them at risk for traumatically bonding to an unhealthy partner.
Jane described her experience of being alone this way:

Any time I was alone as a young girl, or even now, I had to find something to do, or a way not to feel. I would masturbate, or sleep, or eat. I procrastinated with

homework or projects because I just couldn't settle the anxiety inside me.
Time alone permits buried feelings to emerge–feelings that have been ignored for so long that they're overwhelming. When a trauma-bonded woman finds herself alone, she may feel fear, anger, panic, grief, and neediness.

To avoid these feelings, she uses the intensity of a relationship. The relationship becomes her numbing device as she drowns herself in the needs or moods of another person, or the fears the relationship generates. In this way, she borrows a false sense of strength from her relationship. She gathers the ability to function from her relationship. It's the relationship that provides her with energy to get through the day. Her life becomes about maintaining the relationship, and she will frequently neglect friends or children in order to preserve the illusion of love.

If you're in a destructive bond with a partner, you frequently receive negative reactions about your relationship from friends and family. You may notice that you start to hide and cover up your involvement with a particular person, or find yourself constantly defending your partner to others. While this is happening, your shame and isolation grows. You may notice that you believe the false promises you get from your partner. As you tell a friend about something your partner has done, you may notice that you feel horrified, or your friend does, yet you cannot break free from the relationship.

If you answer "yes" to any of the following questions, you may be at risk for traumatic bonding.

- I am drawn to partners who demand sex from me.
- I try to be understood by my partner even when he or she doesn't care.
- I am unable to attract a healthy partner who could be good for me.
- I go to any length to help a person who I know is not healthy for me.
- I think my relationship would end if we stopped having sex for a period of time.
- I want to get away from my partner immediately after we are sexual together.
- I am afraid of my partner.
- I have trouble protecting myself when my partner sexually approaches me.
- I try to change my partner into someone who won't be abusive to me.
- I don't trust my partner, but I can't leave the relationship.

Notice the thread of fear in these questions. With a trauma bond, sexual arousal and fear coexist. The neural pathway for fear and the pathway for pleasure are the strongest, most dynamic pathways in the human brain. Both neural pathways are designed for human protection–one indicates danger, the other insures procreation. When these powerful pathways are jointly activated, the fear center in the brain, the amygdyla, signals to release adrenaline while the pleasure center releases feel-good hormones. The body is overloaded with chemicals designed for contradicting purposes. It's overstimulating and overwhelming.

If this happens in childhood, the tender young brain and body can become attached to the combination of fear and pleasure. They become fused. Sexual arousal and fear go together, and the signaling of one indicates the need for the other. Therefore, in adulthood an automatic reaction to stress or anxiety can be sexual arousal. If a relationship that you are in produces fear or stress, it can actually serve to bond you closer to the destructive person. While this isn't logical, in the bodymind of a trauma survivor it doesn't have to be. Sex and fear are merged. Bonding, then, becomes a dangerous endeavor. In *The Betrayal Bond,* Carnes describes this automatic reaction in the following words: "... adult survivors of abusive and dysfunctional families struggle with bonds that are rooted in their own betrayal experiences."[10]

Maria's sexual relationship with Jerry is a good example of a trauma bond. The foundation of their relationship was built on sexual intensity that contained an element of fear. Jerry's drug addiction left Maria constantly nervous, on guard, and afraid of what might happen next. She couldn't count on Jerry to meet his promises or commitments to her. He always had good excuses for his lack of availability, and Maria's desperate need for love kept her believing his words even though his behavior didn't correspond.

After a fight one night, just two months after they began dating, Jerry slashed the tires on her car. While this seems extreme for most people, Maria felt she had provoked his anger and strangely deserved the violence to her car. She justified and minimized Jerry's behavior as a way to stay attached to him. Over time, her shame grew. She couldn't tell her friends about the relationship because it was too humiliating. She hid from the exact nature of her bond to Jerry. Although she tried to leave Jerry several times, it took three years to finally sever the bond. When she finally left, she had the support of her therapist and a 12-step group. She also read about her addiction. Even with all these efforts, her struggle to leave Jerry caused immense suffering and self-doubt.

Before, each time they broke up, Maria went into withdrawal. She craved Jerry like an alcoholic needs a drink. She would return to him, and they would experience intense feelings of euphoria and honeymoon-like joy. Maria felt so sure each time that it would be different and they could make it work. But within a matter of weeks, the same destructive patterns would again emerge, leaving her in despair and shame. The cycle repeated itself over and over. Her bond with Jerry could have continued for many more years. In the words of Kasl, "Addictive behavior keeps shame constantly recycling..."[11] Maria worked to break the cycle of shame and addiction by immersing herself in the recovery process.

Removing oneself from a trauma bond is extremely difficult. A woman's entire system is designed for connection and bonding. When this delicate neurochemistry is fused with a fear response, the presence of anxiety and stress in a relationship feels normal. It feels like love. The intensity of the fear response mixed with a bonding response is the most powerful marriage of hormones and can create a solid bond between two people, even though the bond is destructive.

Without healing the original childhood betrayal, a woman will not be able to exit a trauma bond. Carnes explains how a trauma bond is in fact a betrayal bond. *Like gravity, you may defy it for a while, but ultimately it will pull you back. You cannot walk away from it. Time will not heal it. Burying yourself in compulsive and addictive behaviors will bring no relief, just more pain. Being crazy will not make it better. No amount of therapy, long-term or short-term, will help without confronting it. Your ability to have a spiritual experience will be impaired. Any form of conversion or starting over only postpones the inevitable. And there is no credit for feeling sorry for yourself. You must acknowledge, understand, and come to terms with the relationship.*[12]

Like Maria, Brooklyn's relationship with her husband is also a trauma bond. Their fighting creates fear for Brooklyn, yet she remains attached to him. In fact, the attachment seems solidified by the intensity of their fighting. Brooklyn's brain is addicted to the chemicals released during conflict, and they merge with the chemicals designed for bonding and pleasure. Brooklyn continues to gain awareness of this difficult relationship in therapy, but as with any trauma bond, the process is slow.

Barbara

You may remember Barbara's story from Chapter One. Her relationship with Jerome illustrates the intricate dance between erotic rage and a trauma bond. Jerome was extremely seductive and charismatic and Barbara liked him right away. She wanted to impress him, so she invited him to her home one day after work, put on some romantic music, and served a nice bottle of wine. In the course of this first evening together, they learned they shared a love for jazz, rhythm and blues. Barbara was hooked. She felt chemically drawn to Jerome in a powerful way. Part of the allure for her was Jerome's ethnicity. He was black, and she found the color of his skin exotic, risky, and daring. Interracial dating was taboo in her family.

Jerome lived with his mother in an impoverished part of town. When Barbara visited, Jerome warned his friends not to damage her car. This element of danger intrigued Barbara even more, increasing her sense of excitement and adventure. For Barbara, Jerome represented the thrill of the unknown. She always felt on edge with him, never knowing what might happen next. She ignored the red flags–his living arrangement, drug and alcohol abuse, and gang activity. To someone without an addictive need for sex and love, Jerome may have appeared dangerous. To Barbara, he was enticing.

Barbara excused Jerome's excessive drinking, and on several occasions let him borrow her car. After he wrecked the car, Barbara had to tell her father. Barbara's father raged about Jerome, calling him a "nigger." But still, her father had her car repaired. Barbara's father was a bigot. His racist anger helped Barbara make sense, much later in life, of her attraction to Jerome. In part, Barbara's erotic rage toward her father came out in her choice of companions. She could make her father angry by dating a black man.

On a deep level this was Barbara's way of kicking her father out of her life without really doing it. Barbara's father maintained his position in her life by rescuing her. He fixed her car. He needed to be Barbara's hero and, on some level, the only man in her life. If he had left Barbara to fix the car on her own, she would have had to deal with the consequences of her behavior. She may have been able to get angry with Jerome, or hold him accountable for the damage to her car. Instead, she felt protective of Jerome and shielded him from her father's racist wrath. Afterward she became even more drawn to him.

Barbara was obsessed with Jerome. She craved him all the time. Sometimes Jerome would make plans to see her and not show up. He came by her place randomly when he felt like it. To make it easier for him, Barbara gave him a key. When Barbara was at work she tried to find excuses to see Jerome. She timed her breaks to coincide with his and met him in the cafeteria for lunch. Jerome never encouraged Barbara's visits at work. He would say hi then leave the room or become disengaged. Barbara had a sense that she was being intrusive but didn't care. She had to see him. Her need for Jerome was beyond her control. Barbara gave all her power to Jerome, which left him in control of the relationship.

In many ways, Barbara was repeating her traumatic childhood with Jerome. Each time she went to him, she repeated the early abandonment feelings she endured as a child when her father nearly died. She felt neglected and lonely with Jerome, just as she felt as a young child when her father was taken to the hospital. Barbara had no inner resources to cope with her intolerable feelings of abandonment. She began bringing different men home from the hospital to have sex with her. This behavior created more stress for her, as there was always a chance Jerome might catch her with a lover, even though he never did.

However, Barbara's body suffered the consequences of her out-of-control sexual and romantic behavior. She contracted an STD, and terminated a pregnancy knowing in her most sane moments that having a baby would be a terrible mistake with the level of abuse in the relationship with Jerome. Barbara knows she's lucky. It was the beginning of legalized abortion, and although she went alone and suffered the ordeal without help, she realizes how easily she could have died from a self-terminated pregnancy.

When Barbara visited Israel after graduation, she knew in some way it was her only chance to break ties with Jerome. Her father knew it, too. Again, he used his power and money to rescue his daughter. Barbara left, and although her time away served to separate her from Jerome, she still kept a secret spot in her heart for him. Now, sixty-five years old and three husbands later, Barbara is sad as she tells her story. She's been in therapy for thirty years and maintains a professional life, yet she hasn't been able to break the obsession with Jerome. He still haunts her thoughts.

It's considered "euphoric recall" when a person romanticizes past relationships, hangs onto only the good parts, repressing the bad. In euphoric recall, memories produce wonderful feelings of warmth and pleasure. The memories can cause a person to return to highly destructive relationships. In Barbara's case, euphoric recall plays a part in her inability to let go of Jerome and be fully present to her current partner. She and Jerome are periodically in touch with each other by phone, just enough to keep Barbara in fantasy about who he is.

Barbara's trauma bond with Jerome is an example of what Carnes describes in *The Betrayal Bond*–no amount of time can break a betrayal bond. It happens when an individual bonds to someone abusive. In Barbara's case, it was her father. Now she faces the painful reality that past wounds are still running her life. For Barbara to be whole she must first let go of Jerome, and then emotionally let go of her father.

Damaged Dreams

Addictive relationships take an incredible amount of time and energy to maintain. While it's healthy for a couple to make their relationship a priority and spend time nurturing it, it takes two fairly healthy individuals to achieve this delicate balance. Addictive relationships involve two people who are not whole. Each person looks to the relationship to provide a sense of well-being. Addictive relationships can become all-consuming and inhibit each partner from reaching his or her full potential.

As a result of early childhood trauma, a woman enters a relationship with a fragmented sense of herself. Her brain has been altered from trauma. Distortions occur in the cognitive processes involved in planning, dreaming, and thinking. She has trouble knowing her hopes and dreams. For abuse survivors, the capacity to dream has been damaged. Dreaming and hoping are the ways humans design themselves and their lives. Without the ability to dream or hope, a woman is often without a mission for her life. The sad result can be that a woman lives her life in reaction to the needs and wants of others without the internal or external structures in place to make her own decisions, identify her own wants, or recognize her own needs. Regardless of how her life may look on the outside, she feels empty and useless on the inside.

Without the ability to dream, a woman is at risk for addictive relationships. In fact, her only "dream" may be about having the perfect relationship, which may include having the perfect body, hair, or personality. The pursuit of this dream requires emotional, spiritual, and physical energy. For a sex and love addict, it takes over her life. The sacrifice she makes for her addiction is a large one. She's robbed of a chance to design a life that is fulfilling. She aches with emptiness and a sense of wasted potential. Herein lies the ultimate betrayal of an addiction to love and sex–a woman's dreams are damaged and her heart is broken. The pain of lost loves is nothing compared to the pain of living her life with a chronic sense of emptiness and waste. Understood in this way, we can see sex and love addiction as a measure of self-abuse

Ready to Heal

Confronting the reality of your childhood abuse and your cultural heritage as a woman means reconnecting with tender feelings of anger, pain, and shame. Denial, in many forms, has been the shield that protected you from painful inner wounds. But as you face the unmanageability of your addictive use of relationships you acquire new eyes. The denial about childhood begins to crack and the myth that "wasn't it like this for everyone" crumbles.

Advertising and media that create an impossible standard of beauty now seem offensive. As you face addictive relationships and the emotional starvation you have endured, it becomes more difficult to use a relationship to avoid the emptiness in your life. You begin to know that addictive relationships perpetuate a form of violence to your soul and keep your original trauma alive. Emotional deprivation is no longer acceptable and you become ready to explore your inner world and the pain you have been medicating with sex and love.

Chapter Seven
Healing Addictive Romantic Behavior

Relationship addiction–as with all unhealthy dependencies–is an attempt to heal our perceived deficits through something outside ourselves, when in reality our inner sense of emptiness is a spiritual void.
Stephanie Covington, *Leaving the Enchanted Forest*[1]

Healing compulsive romantic and sexual behavior is a journey of courage and faith. Courage to face feelings and memories you've been avoiding for a long time; and faith that after doing so there will be a better life waiting for you. It would be nice to anticipate a reward. Humans need rewards. We are pleasure-oriented. But right now it's probably difficult for you to imagine a reward that isn't part of your addiction and fantasy. A list of healthy rewards might even appear boring and undesirable. Rewards will come, and when they do, you will choose them according to your healthy needs and desires.

The steps outlined in this chapter provide a guide to start your healing journey. At first they may sound simple. They are. However, you're the one who must take the steps. No one can do it for you. Each measure you take to heal your addiction is your decision. It's worth considering very carefully. In order to succeed, you must be very clear about why you want to stop your addictive behavior. It's helpful to have a goal in mind. What inspires you to change? If it's simply that you want to stop hurting, that may not be enough motivation. Your brain is accustomed to high levels of pain and adrenaline, and the moment you feel a bit of relief you may find yourself returning to old destructive habits. It's not uncommon to start out strong on a healing journey, inspired by a particularly dreadful sexual binge or damaging relationship, only to find yourself once again drowning in shame and despair from another form of the disease.

What are some reasons women want to change? The following examples are from others who have entered the sexual recovery process with no guarantee of what their lives might look like after the healing process. Instead of clear outcomes, they had firm goals. Their ambitions kept them motivated when the journey got difficult.

I didn't want to raise my children the way I was raised...with a stream of different men through the house. It terrified me when I saw myself repeating my mother's habits.

I knew that if I entered into another relationship with someone, I would hurt him. I couldn't stand the thought of seeing another person aching because of what I had done. I hurt some really nice people. It had to stop.

I got tired of living in ambivalence about my sexual orientation. I had been in relationships with men and women without feeling satisfied. After a while, I realized I was hiding from making commitments by not choosing my sexual preference. Deep down, I think I knew I was heterosexual, but I was afraid to admit my choice for fear that I would have to live with my decision, and I might get bored or be wrong. I entered sexual recovery because, in my heart, I knew I wanted something more for myself.

I got scared that something was really wrong with me, and I could never love someone. The thought of dying alone began to bother me.

These women each had unique reasons that directed their recovery journey. They took on recovery as a mission. For some of you, making this decision may be the first time you have created a clear goal for yourself. The legacy of abuse may have left you without a life purpose. Reaching clarity now about why you want to recover from this addiction is an empowering step toward regaining your life, reclaiming damaged dreams, and finding the joy and peace that you deserve.

Consider answering the following questions:

1. When I am in my disease (when my addict is running the show) what kind of person am I?
   (selfish, greedy, dependent, needy, insatiable, hungry, lonely, afraid, etc.)

_____

_____

_____

2. Who am I really?
   (loving, generous, happy, hopeful, focused, intelligent, kind, playful, etc.)

_____

_____

_____

Pick the words which best describe you and add words that you feel complete the picture of who you are. Think of your answers like this: Who were you before abuse changed you? What kind of child were you? Share these thoughts with your therapist, 12-step group, or a trusted friend.

Now consider who you would like to be. Let your imagination play. Think of your favorite three words from above, and use them to guide you in creating a new definition of who you will be without your addiction.

3. Who do I want to be?

_____

_____

_____

_____

Now, imagine what stands in your way of being who you want to be? List at least five things that could create distractions or problems for you in your healing journey. Some ideas may include losing focus on your mission, missing therapy appointments, skipping group support, turning to alcohol or drugs to numb painful feelings, etc.

1. _____

_____

2. _____

_____

3. _____

_____

4. _____

_____

5. _____

_____

Healing Brings Vulnerability

Addiction has served to keep you insulated from how terribly vulnerable you are. When you decide to stop using your addiction to hide from yourself, you will encounter feelings that seem larger than life. Waves of fear, grief, and anger will wash over you at unexpected times. It will seem as if you're drowning in the feelings. It will be terrifying. Maria recalls the following:

I was alone in bed one night for the first time since beginning my withdrawal period. I felt so small, so little. Although I was twenty-nine and I had a young child sleeping in the next room, I felt totally incapable of getting through the night alone. And then I remembered feeling this way as a little girl and asking my mother if I could sleep with a doll or stuffed animal. She said no. When I asked why, she explained coldly that I would become dependent on it and be unable to fall asleep alone. So now, here I was, a grown woman, and I was unable to fall asleep alone. My little girl fears and needs were still with me. My mother's attempt to make me strong didn't work. So I got out of bed, grabbed an extra pillow, and hugged it tightly until I could stop shaking. Tears came and I cried deep sobs into my pillow, muffling my sounds from my child in the next room. I craved someone to make it all OK. But I was alone and I knew this was my pain to heal.

To begin healing, you must be willing to face tender feelings like Maria's. These feelings are fueling your addiction. And your addiction keeps these feelings hidden from your awareness, making sure that you're unable to heal them. You're in a cycle that's keeping you sick. Breaking the cycle means letting go of destructive habits and/or people. Letting go hurts. Even if you're letting go of painful patterns, you'll feel a loss. There will be rage and grief.

Jane remembers when she decided she must leave a particularly destructive relationship. She knew she had to get out, yet every bit of her hated the idea of leaving him. She cried the day she walked out of his apartment telling him, "I have to go…you're no good for me." Although she was the one to leave, she struggled with horrible abandonment feelings. She felt rage, and her impaired thinking told her that if she had only tried harder, then she could still be with him. It's torture to let go of this addiction. There's no pain like it.

Awareness: A First Step

There's no right or wrong way to let go of sex and love addiction. But before change can happen, you must first be fully aware of what you're doing. Awareness means you honestly take a look at your behavior and decide if you can embrace the fact that you have an addiction. This is not easy as there can be shame attached to the concept of addiction. However, it's only a name. It's not who you are. The name will guide you in your desire to change. A name directs the healing process. A name is not meant to be confining. It's a way to identify your problem, gain power over it, and begin to heal in ways that have worked for other women before you. Here are some of the ways others first started.

Maria

I remember going to my therapist and saying, "I think I'm addicted to men, or romance, or something. Something is wrong and I don't know what to do." Although my therapist didn't understand me at the time, I felt stronger by saying it out aloud. The following week, I found a flyer at a woman's group I was attending. It said "If your relationships look like train wrecks, if you feel empty without a man, or if you wonder if other women experience this too, give us a call." The next day, I called the number on the bottom of the page and, miraculously, it

was the 12-step fellowship of Sex and Love Addicts Anonymous.
I remember going to my first meeting. I went alone and I was scared, but as I listened to the women sharing their stories, I felt safe and warm. It's like I had come home. Never before had I experienced women talking about my life without even knowing me. Afterward, I told my therapist about my realizations and this amazing fellowship of women, and together we began to learn about the addiction and develop a treatment plan.

Heather

My therapist listened to me describe the situation I was in with Mark, and she told me I was a sex and love addict. I was shocked. I had heard of this addiction in other 12-step meetings, but hearing it from my therapist made it real. She told me I would have to give up the fantasy of Mark, go to an SLAA meeting, and begin a withdrawal period. At first I was angry because I already felt the burden of treating my eating disorder. But I knew she was right. Inside it was a kind of relief to know that there was a name for what I was doing with men, and that I might be able to find another way to live.

Miranda

I went to a treatment center for my cocaine addiction. While I was there, I learned from the team of specialists that I was a sex addict. They told me I shouldn't date for a while. But when I left the center, I returned to my boyfriend. I couldn't imagine sobriety without him.

But I did find a therapist who specialized in sex and love addiction and began telling her the truth about myself. She encouraged me to attend meetings for sex and love addicts in addition to Narcotics Anonymous meetings.

Tori

After I had been sober for six months from alcohol, my therapist told me I was a sex addict. I thought she was crazy. I wasn't a sex addict....I was just popular! But in that session, as we reviewed my history, the consequences of my compulsive sexual behavior wasn't pretty. They included herpes, a date rape, and dangerous men. My denial began to crack and I knew she was right. I knew I had to face the reality that my sexual behavior was killing me, and I couldn't trust myself.

Barbara

Walking alone in a vineyard one afternoon, I reviewed my sexual history and realized that it was no different than my addiction to food. I was using sex to hide my feelings and it wasn't working anymore. I was still lonely, achy, and far from respecting myself. I decided that day to go to an SLAA meeting and find out if there was a way for me to heal.

A Second Step

When you've decided that indeed you're addicted to sex, love, and relationships–and you no longer want to be–you've made a powerful first step toward a new life. Denial is no longer going to serve you. It won't be fun anymore to repeat your destructive habits. You're too smart.

You may experience the old saying "ignorance is bliss" with new appreciation. You may long for the days when you could act out sexually without wondering why. But now you know where it leads. You can't hide from yourself anymore. It's no longer OK to think that what you're doing is harmless, natural, or as one woman put it:

I always thought I was just more sexual than everyone else, and it was a special gift I had. I felt unique and used astrology, the moon cycles, and new age thinking to justify my behavior. When my therapist first introduced the concept of addiction, I was enraged, but part of me also felt seen. For the first time I saw that my sex life might not be exactly what I thought it was, and I felt some hope that maybe I could change.

With new insight comes a healthy desire for change. The desire for change flows from a place deep inside you that knows you deserve more from life. It comes from faith that shame and despair aren't your legacy. You're meant to be happy. You're designed for joy. But in order to strengthen the desire for change, you need to take action. In order to stop an addiction, you must put down the drug.

With a substance addition, such as alcohol, cocaine, or nicotine, you're either using the drug or you aren't. There's no middle ground. But with love and sex addiction, it's much more difficult to determine how to give up the drug. Since sexuality and human relationships are a healthy, necessary part of life, deciding what behavior you must stop isn't always clear. As you decide how to proceed, remind yourself of your goals. What do you want to achieve? Who do you want to be? Remember, the only thing standing in the way of you having the life you want is your disease, and the only way to heal is to begin treating this addiction.

What Do I Have to Look Forward to?

Your disillusionment with compulsive sex and love is steering you in the direction of more authentic forms of intimacy and connection. Although it's been twisted by abuse and addiction, the yearning for connection that you feel isn't misguided. Searching for love directs you to find a solution to the damage of sex and love addiction. It's from a place of self-love that you find the desire to change. As you embark on a sexual healing journey, love can be your guide. Not addictive, craving love, but a true desire for something better for yourself.

Even if you don't yet know exactly what you want your life to look like without sex and love addiction, the fact that you're ready to change sets positive principles in motion. Certain benefits will emerge during your sexual healing journey. These benefits are unique to women who seriously take on the challenge to address this addiction and follow certain guidelines. Here are some of the benefits that you can anticipate.

- You will instinctively know when and how to avoid certain situations that put you at risk. Decision making will become easier. You will have less confusion.

- You will learn to trust and accept others as you learn to trust and accept yourself.

- You will learn to take responsibility for your own well-being and happiness, putting self-responsibility in place of self-abuse.

- As you surrender, moment by moment, your obsession with romance and sexual intrigue, you will develop a stronger spirituality. Spirituality, as distinct and separate from religion, involves a certain knowing that you are no longer alone in your efforts to heal from past abuse and from your addiction.

- You will begin to know peace. Solitude will become nourishing rather than frightening.

- Your shame and perfectionism will diminish, leaving room for authentic feelings of joy, pleasure, humility, and pain.

- You will become honest expressing who you are in relationships with others. You will experience real intimacy.

- Sexual feelings and expressions will emerge as a result of honest sharing, commitment, and trust in a relationship.

Intervention: Taking Back Your Life and Power

Making the decision to change your addictive romantic patterns requires careful consideration. The next step is the most difficult thing you may ever do. Admitting that you have an addiction means you must consider relinquishing your drug. Addictions don't heal by themselves. More time, the right books, good intentions, or your next vacation won't cure this disease. Healing sex and love addiction requires *action and effort.*

The first step is to identify a problematic behavior and stop. Some women stop cold-turkey. Others stop more gradually. The choice is yours. But you must realize that when you decide to stop a particular pattern, it's going to hurt. You've been medicating your brain with sexual and romantic behavior. You've created a whole life to support your addictive habits.

Stopping will not come naturally, and at times you'll find yourself discouraged, afraid, and angry. The decision must be yours, because if you do it for someone else (a partner, a therapist, or a family member), it will be easy to blame them when it gets too hard. This is your life and only you can make the decision to start healing.

The decision to heal this disease means saying "no" to your addiction. You're saying that you want your life back. No longer will you let the pursuit of a new relationship fill your thoughts and time. You won't use sex as a way to escape what you're feeling. You'll stop using people as drugs. In essence, you'll reclaim your life. You will take back the power that your disease has stolen from you.

You'll learn to cultivate authentic power that comes from dignity and self-respect, rather than false power that comes from a quick fix, the next conquest, or a sexual high.

Entering Withdrawal

Suppose your addiction takes the form of meeting people online and secretly sharing sexual fantasies. Then beginning recovery means you stop. Suppose your addiction takes the form of having an affair. Then to start recovery, you stop the affair. Suppose you're addicted to one particular person and the relationship has become destructive. Then healing means you take time away from this person. Perhaps you're masturbating compulsively, but not interested is having sex with your partner. Then you stop masturbating. Suppose you're sexually anorexic. Then recovery means you decide to listen to what your body is telling you and find treatment.

When you choose to stop your compulsive use of sex and romance, you will enter a withdrawal period. Withdrawal is different for each woman. No woman does it the same. When you start withdrawal, you essentially take a step toward sobriety. You decide which actions leave you feeling shame and despair, and you leave them alone. At first, you may only stop behavior that's clearly a problem, learning as the process unfolds that there are other behaviors that also need to go. Consider the following:

Maria

When Maria first entered sexual recovery, she didn't identify her relationship with Jerry as part of her main addiction. She thought she could still keep Jerry, but stop seeing other men. So her first step toward sobriety was the decision to be faithful to Jerry. Her therapist asked her if she planned to stop flirting and meeting men. Maria felt this wasn't necessary.

But within weeks, she found herself on the phone with a man she had met at the grocery store. And there she was with another secret and a chance to be unfaithful to Jerry. Maria had to reassess her bottom-line behavior. She took flirting and meeting men off her list of acceptable behavior because she realized that by flirting she put herself at risk. Part of Maria's disease included an inability to say "no" to a man who wanted her. So she needed to stop inviting men with her engaging smile, eye contact, and suggestive clothing. Maria faced changing her entire personality.

Heather
When Heather first set a bottom line, it involved cutting off all contact with Mark and entering a period of no dating. In order to do this, she had to stop the fantasy that Mark needed an explanation. Every part of her wanted to discuss this with Mark and give him the opportunity to understand. What she was doing was looking for Mark to change her mind. Her therapist assured her that he needed no explanation, and that her addict simply wanted another opportunity for contact with him.

Tori
Tori faced withdrawal from a trauma bond with James. She knew the relationship could no longer be part of a healthy life. Her therapist steadily helped Tori deal with the reality of her addiction to James, and supported Tori's involvement in the 12-step community. Tori also spent time away in a treatment setting designed to help her heal childhood wounding. Tori's deep emotional work began to pay off. As her sober time increased, she began to like herself.

At the same time, her tolerance for James and his abuse decreased. Step by step, she learned to set sexual boundaries with him, and each time he ignored them, a part of her left the relationship. It took a full year, but eventually she said goodbye to James. Tori remembers feeling "a huge pit in my stomach...a hole that felt infinite," but she had faith that James could no longer be her focus. At that point, Tori entered into an agreement with her sponsor and therapist to avoid flirting, dating, and sex for a time period.

Sometimes withdrawal is not a choice. It may be forced on you. In Brooklyn's case, her husband returned to treatment a second time for drug addiction. She faced being by herself for a month. She came to therapy plagued with symptoms of withdrawal. She reported feelings of high anxiety, sleeplessness, and complete devotion to her husband. This is the same woman who only weeks before had been having sex with other men without her husband knowing. With her husband away, however, she lost the desire for other men. She only wanted him.

Martha
For Martha, her withdrawal began when she discovered her husband's sexual addiction. Although she knew something was wrong in her marriage, she had no idea he was sexually acting out. She knew he kept long hours at work, but she assumed he would change on his own. She thought if she were prettier and nicer,

he would spend more time at home with her and their kids.

By the time she learned of his behavior, her husband had put them $150,000 in debt with his use of prostitutes and strip clubs. He was fired from his job, and without an income, was forced to tell his wife the truth. They decided he needed to go into treatment. Martha suddenly found herself alone and afraid. With her husband away, she faced the truth about her low self-esteem and her unhealthy dependency on the relationship. She spent many sleepless nights before she found a therapist who could help her. In therapy, she learned she was addicted to her partner and deprived of love. She faced treating her own addiction to her husband. Her therapist encouraged her to attend a 12-step meeting for women in relationship with sex addicts called COSA.

What does withdrawal feel like?

Choosing to stop addictive romantic behavior means you enter a withdrawal period. You may be familiar with the concept of withdrawal from knowledge of other addictions. Sex and love are similar. Because romantic behavior is neurochemical, your brain has become addicted to the high of sex, intrigue, lying, cheating, arousal, and fear. Your brain uses the hormones that come from addictive relationships to feel OK. When you enter withdrawal, you're taking these brain chemicals away. It's like taking away cigarettes from a nicotine addict.

When you decide to enter withdrawal, you face more than a broken heart or the loss of an opportunity to feel high. In essence, you face a kind of death–the death of your double life, your second self, your addict. You face the death of a fantasy, the dream that you're in the perfect relationship, or if you just try again, you'll find Mr. Right. Your addiction is like another personality. Its sole purpose is to provide you an escape into love and sex. Without it, you're left not knowing who you are or if you can survive. You meet terror, grief, and anger. You face incredible vulnerability.

Without your addiction, you feel irritable, tired, hungry, lonely, scared, and confused. You may have headaches and stomachaches. There will be times you can't sleep. You may wish to sleep all the time and not face the world. In withdrawal, you begin to feel the original terror of your early childhood abuse and psychological isolation. Here is what some women found during the early part of withdrawal:

Some days, I didn't trust myself driving the car. I felt shaky and small behind the wheel, and literally had to turn around and go home.

What this woman is describing is the very real fear that comes in early withdrawal. She no longer has hormones in her system that give her a false sense of being OK or being a grown up. She returns to a younger part of herself. She meets her childhood pain and fear. Although she's in a woman's body, she's still a little girl. No little girl should be driving a car. Some days in early withdrawal are like this. Driving a car is not a good idea, going to work may not be possible, and basic life skills become terribly challenging.

It felt like a sculptor was taking a chisel to my head and chipping away at a shell. It hurt. I've never felt such torture. My whole persona was breaking. Without being able to flirt, I didn't know how to behave. Do I smile? Do I look away? Where do I focus?

Entering withdrawal is equivalent to taking off your clothing. You remove your cover. Some women describe feeling like a raw nerve in a wind storm. You remove the layers of behavior that have been designed to attract your next romance or keep your partner happy.

I couldn't sleep...I was so afraid at night. I was sure that someone was coming to get me or would hurt me.

This woman is describing the night terrors that may come in early withdrawal. For many abuse survivors, nighttime was not a safe time to be a child. Terrible things happened at night. Maggie remembers her parents fighting at night. One time, she saw her father brutally attack her mother. She felt too scared to move. She couldn't do anything to help her mother and was terrified her mother might die. She froze. Now in withdrawal, youthful feelings come rushing into her mind at night and she finds herself unable to sleep.

Like Maggie, Barbara couldn't sleep at night during early withdrawal. She felt so afraid that she repeatedly got out of bed to check the doors, making sure they were locked. She kept her windows sealed and closed, and left lights on throughout the house. She watched TV until she was so tired she could no longer keep her eyes open. When she woke in the morning, the TV was still on.

It's common in early withdrawal to replace the missing romantic high with food. Eating sweets replaces some of the hormones that are lost when a woman decides to give up sex or dating. One woman says, "When I started withdrawing from sex, I started eating sweets at night and gained 20 pounds really fast."

Some women encounter anger in withdrawal. Consider the following examples:

I found myself irritable and unable to play with my children. I just wanted to stay in bed all day.

For mothers at home with children, entering withdrawal is like living in hell. Her children have legitimate needs from her, but she can barely meet her own. When a woman enters withdrawal, it takes amazing energy to complete basic life skills. Tasks like cleaning, working, hygiene, and eating become a chore. If a woman must also care for children, she faces incredible difficulty in withdrawal.

For me, it was like a cold bucket of ice water on my head first thing in the morn-

ing. I felt cold, achy, lonely, and angry.

I remember the first three days in withdrawal were kind of OK. I kept thinking…hmm, what's the big deal? Then it hit. On day four, I couldn't get out of bed. I called my therapist and she said go for a walk and then take a hot bath. I was furious! How was that going to help? But I did it. And the next day, I did it again. And day by day, piece by piece, moment by moment, I learned new tools to deal with the dark craving in my soul.

This story reveals a common reaction to early withdrawal. Due to heightened hormones that come from leaving a destructive relationship, the brain can still feel high for a few days, enjoying fantasies of revenge or hope that the other person is hurting or will come crawling back to you. When these neurochemicals calm down and reality sets in, the pain begins. It's at this moment that your withdrawal truly kicks in and you'll need to call on your resources for help.

This woman's therapist responded beautifully. A walk was designed to get blood flowing to her brain and help with the withdrawal feelings. A bath soothes the skin, and can be a type of all-body hug. In this way, her therapist addressed her touch needs and her brain needs. Although it wasn't what she wanted to hear, this particular addict had wonderful support for early withdrawal.

However, you and your therapist need to be aware that a bath can also be a trigger for an addict during early recovery. Many women learned to experience sexual pleasure as children in the bathtub. For this reason, non-sexual massage may be a better solution for touch deprivation in early withdrawal.

Why do I need to face withdrawal?

When I first began withdrawal, I started crying a lot. I was sure when the crying started it wouldn't stop. I think I was crying years' worth of tears, and incredible waves of fear came with the sadness. These feelings were terrible.

Withdrawal is a critical part of recovery. Without using your drug of choice, you come face to face with grief. You will feel defective, unlovable, unworthy, and broken. These lies will seem real and you'll feel terrible. You might say to yourself, *No wonder I'm an addict.* At times, your addiction will look appealing compared to the darkness you're facing now. But by facing grief, you face your negative beliefs. These are the lies you inherited culturally and in an abusive family. As they are revealed, you have the opportunity to heal them. You can't heal what you can't see. Your addiction has kept you a stranger to these lies. In withdrawal, these lies will be unveiled and four benefits will occur.

- Your addictive behavior will no longer fuel the negative beliefs that you've inherited.
- Without addictive acting out, your negative beliefs grow weak.
- By simply avoiding your addictive behavior, you take concrete steps to

disarm these beliefs.
* Without a negative belief system, there's less fuel for addiction and the process gets easier.

Facing the range of behavior that has been part of your sex and love addiction can be very discouraging. You may discover that the clothes in your closet are all designed to attract sexual attention. Or that your previous ability to be helpful and available was a covert way to entangle a love interest. It may seem that your whole personality is being challenged. But stay focused. Remember your goals. Trust that you will make it through and a better life is waiting for you.

Withdrawing from a Trauma Bond

Remember there are different ways to enter into a withdrawal period. You can try the cold-turkey approach and cease all behavior that could be addictive. Or you can whittle out one behavior at a time to try to heal your patterns. In my experience, an addictive relationship that is also a trauma bond is the most difficult withdrawal. Stopping all addictive behavior hurts, but since women form a sense of self inside a relationship, deciding to leave a romantic relationship is like losing an arm or a leg. Few women elect to do this willingly. Usually, something terrible occurs that forces a woman out of a traumatic relationship. Her children may be threatened or her partner may leave.

To illustrate the slow process of withdrawing from a trauma bond, let's consider Maria's story. In Maria's case, she first entered withdrawal still hoping to have a relationship with Jerry. After some time in therapy, she realized she needed more support in order to recover from this disease. She found the program of sex and love addicts anonymous. When she began SLAA, her early definition of sobriety included no flirting and not meeting other men. She was determined to be a better partner to Jerry. Incidentally, Maria also decided not to drink alcohol for a year when she began this process. She didn't know if alcohol was making her addiction to sex stronger, but she wanted to learn.

So she began attending 12-step meetings for alcoholics and also for sex and love addicts. She also maintained weekly therapy appointments. She was working hard and learning a lot about her addiction. For a while, her relationship with Jerry improved. She had less shame because she wasn't carrying secrets and Jerry seemed to enjoy her renewed attention toward him. But soon he began to withdraw from the intensity of the relationship and Maria began to suffer.

It became harder to stay sober. The more Jerry withdrew, the more I craved him. He would pull away and deny that it was happening, and I would feel crazy. I found myself wanting to find another lover to make the pain go away.

With the help of her therapist and sponsor, Maria decided she needed to consider leaving Jerry. The relationship with him was creating too much pain for her to remain in recovery. But she wanted to try one last thing. She had learned of a group for couples called Recovering Couples Anonymous and wanted to try it with Jerry before giving up. Jerry agreed to go to the group with Maria, and the two began attending meetings together. In the RCA meetings, they shared their pain and struggle with other couples. They also listened to the honest sharing of other couples with similar problems. Maria found the group to be an incredible source of strength. Jerry, however, was not so sure. He was encouraged by another man in the group to explore the possibility that he might have a sexual addiction. Maria had suspected that Jerry was a sex addict, but she had learned in her 12-step meetings not to diagnose another addict. She was relieved when the suggestion came from a member of their group who was also a sex addict.

Maria was encouraged to attend a COSA group meeting. Although Jerry did not heed the recommendation to explore his sexual addiction, Maria attended the meeting and found wonderful information that "provided the missing piece!"
She not only was attending SLAA, AA and RCA, but also COSA. Her recovery began to truly take off. She learned to set boundaries with Jerry, and how to handle sexual feelings that seemed to come from nowhere. She learned that some of her desire to act out sexually was coming from Jerry. She was carrying sexual rage and arousal that he was unable to identify and manage responsibly. This accounted for part of why she felt so crazy with Jerry.

Steadily, Maria's sense of self-worth began to grow. She started to like herself without constant attention from Jerry. Gradually, she began to detach from him. Little by little, she started creating friendships with women that made her feel good. Her life started to feel better as she returned to graduate school to pursue a degree she wanted. Her ability to be with her child also became stronger. She felt less irritability and less pain.

It took Maria six months from her COSA involvement, and three years from the beginning of her SLAA work to finally leave Jerry. Although she had hoped that RCA would be the glue to keep their relationship together, the outcome was different. Maria learned instead that she didn't have a partner willing to look at himself. In RCA, Maria was able to see the imbalance in their relationship and with the witnessing of others, her denial cracked. She found it increasingly difficult to be seduced by his words, his flattery, and his dramatic efforts to keep her involved with him.

Maria's story is an illustration of how some women cannot begin withdrawal by quitting the disease cold turkey. Jerry was part of her disease, but he was also a significant relationship in her life. Her story also illustrates the importance of support in order to recover. Women do not recover from this disease alone. Initially, they can't see the disease in its many forms. Maria's love and sex addiction had many layers that required much effort to untangle.

Tori and Maria's story are very similar. They both embraced 12-step programs in addition to therapy, to separate from the unhealthy relationships they were in. Like Tori and James, Maria and Jerry were trauma-bonded. If you remember from earlier chapters, Jerry could be violent and unpredictable. In this way, Maria was repeating the abuse she experienced with her father. Jerry could also be seductive and unavailable. For Maria, this combination created just enough hope to keep her, and just enough fear to hook her. Her neural pathways for sexual pleasure and fear were fused in childhood, and in the relationship with Jerry, she found the perfect blend to keep them activated.

Additionally, Maria learned no boundaries in her childhood, making her a perfect partner for a sex addict. Because she had learned to use sex to gain power and attention, she knew how to please a man sexually. Her codependency and sex addiction interacted to create a perfect mix for a trauma bond. Fortunately for Maria, her determination and desire for a better life kept her searching for answers. Her recovery meetings, therapy, and hope moved her toward a withdrawal period. Ultimately she left Jerry, and began a no-dating, no-flirting, and no-sex time period.

What will help me succeed in withdrawal?

Now that you've made the decision to start relational and sexual recovery, there are issues to consider. It's important to set yourself up for success right away. Repeated failures can leave you feeling ashamed and hopeless, adding to your negative belief system. Consider the following:

Find support

As a therapist, I don't recommend withdrawal until certain things are in place for you. This is a painful detoxification process. Withdrawal shocks the brain and puts you in terrible pain. The necessary foundation for success includes:

- Regular, weekly meetings with a trained therapist who understands this disease and can provide structure, comfort, and guidance. If appropriate, biweekly meetings are even better.

- Regular attendance in the 12-step program of SLAA, COSA, Al-Anon, or CODA.

Be aware of your excuses

It's common in early withdrawal for your brain to sabotage your decision to heal. You may find yourself with all kinds of reasons why you simply must indulge in an addictive hit. Here are some of the things you may tell yourself:

- I can't help seeing him again. He works in the same building as I do.
- I have just as much right to be in that meeting (location, function, coffee shop) as he does.
- Why do I have to be the one to suffer withdrawal?
- I haven't seen him/her for a few weeks, so that must mean I'm not addicted and I can start seeing him/her again.
- If I don't tell anyone what I'm doing, then it won't count.

- If I only talk to him on the phone, it won't be the same as having sex with him.
- I can drive by his house (place of work) and it won't trigger me.
- I have to keep my cell phone on all night in case someone needs me.
- I can't change my phone number because it's too much trouble.
- Other addicts may need a withdrawal period, but my addiction isn't as bad as theirs.

Avoid cluttering your days with too much activity

The energy it takes to endure withdrawal is equivalent to working a full-time job. Truthfully, this may be the hardest work you've ever done before. In addition to support from people who understand your undertaking, you must keep the rest of your life simple. You need rest and solitude.

Plan healthy rewards

Freeing yourself from addictive habits takes minute-by-minute effort. Simply not doing it takes tremendous strength. You're living in the present moment for the first time in your life. You will wake in the morning feeling a sense of dread, wondering how you can do another day of this. It's helpful to keep a list of healthy, nurturing activities beside your bed. Look at it first thing and pick an activity to treat yourself with. These may include but are not limited to, taking a walk in a beautiful place, finding time for a nap, enjoying a cup of hot tea, going to a movie, reading a good book, spending time with a pet, drawing or painting, or listening to relaxing music.

Right now, none of these things may sound appealing to you. The only thing that sounds good is contact with your addiction. That's OK. Trust the process. Remember, your addiction never feels good for long. It ends up leaving you feeling alone and ashamed.

Write down the way you felt the last time you acted out

It can be helpful to have a concrete reminder of the last time you experienced terrible feelings because of someone you were addicted to or because of a certain sexual behavior. It's inevitable that you will romanticize your disease. You'll forget how much it hurts. You'll experience cravings. Be ready for this and try to avoid the thinking that you'll be the exception to this rule. One woman kept a description by her bed of the injury she suffered while using her vibrator. She included the humiliation she felt when she had to consult a doctor about her situation. When she felt the need to masturbate, she read this description instead and the craving went away.

Another woman wrote a list of the reasons her last husband was unhealthy for her, including his interest in other women, his abuse of alcohol, and his explosive anger. Each time she experienced the euphoric recall, she read her list.

Regular exercise

Aerobic activity increases blood flow to the brain and creates new neuronal connections. Early in withdrawal there is no energy for exercise, but even a slow walk can help the brain in the detoxification process.

Therapeutic Issues in Withdrawal

When I'm assisting a woman in withdrawal, there are other factors to consider. Abuse has physical consequences that can hinder the success of a withdrawal period. If I see a woman making sincere efforts to start withdrawal and repetitively failing, it could be that her abuse history is emerging too quickly. Due to the chemical changes in the brain, withdrawal brings on a crisis. If you find yourself feeling desperate in withdrawal, discuss the following with your therapist.

Touch deprivation

Touch deprivation becomes a factor when you're abstaining from sexual contact. Frequent, regular massage can become part of the treatment plan to heal the lack of physical affection that lingers from childhood and drives your sexual craving. It's important that the massage has no sexual overtones, and that an appropriate person who understands trauma is chosen.

Like many abuse survivors, you may have a fear of being touched by someone you don't know or aren't having sex with. This is normal. Discuss this with your therapist, and find out who is trained to take special time introducing you to the therapeutic benefits of massage.

Treatment

At times, it's necessary for an individual to spend time in an in-patient setting. Withdrawal may bring up many difficult emotions on a daily basis. Without regular support, you could find yourself considering a time-out from life's daily demands and a desire for more rigorous support. Perhaps you have limited access to a 12-step community or a trained specialist.

The feelings that emerge when you begin to abstain from compulsive behavior can leave you unable to care for yourself. If you have children, they may be at risk. There are many reasons to consider treatment, and more centers are equipped to support women healing from love and sex addiction.

Medication

If you feel suicidal during withdrawal, you're not alone. It may indicate that your brain chemistry is severely compromised and medication can assist your process. Discuss this option with your therapist.

On the Other Side of Withdrawal

When you make it through withdrawal, new self-respect emerges. You've survived an amazing process. You now have new, authentic strength.
One woman explains that

... starting my own business was terrifying, but since I'd made it through with-drawal four years earlier, I knew I could handle it. I knew I could handle any-thing.
There's a confidence that comes from making it through withdrawal. Accomplishment creates a glow that seems to come from deep inside you.

Women who make it through the withdrawal process feel special pride about this healing time. There's nothing else like it for comparison. One woman described it as a "kind of rebirth. Withdrawal was the gestation period and at the end, I had a new me." Jane recalls feeling "radiant. I didn't need makeup any-more to leave my house. I knew I was a lovely person, and that's all that mat-tered." Withdrawal brings back the purity that was taken from you as a child. By entering recovery and completing withdrawal, you reclaim a glorious part of your original self.

It's helpful to have some idea of how long withdrawal needs to last in order to enjoy the benefits. In general, it takes thirty to ninety days to simply get over minute-by-minute agony and craving. This is the time it takes to detox. During the next ninety to one-hundred-eighty days, you will experience some relief from the early symptoms of withdrawal. It will be easier to sleep, work, or care for children. During this time, it's critical to cultivate group support and be regular in therapy because the brain is ready to learn new behaviors. You'll be creating new neural pathways daily ready to form healthy relationships and make room for feelings that have been depressed for years.

In the next six to twelve months, your brain will be ready to rebuild damaged dreams. The second half of the withdrawal year is about reclaiming. The life that was taken from you is yours to retrieve. Withdrawal is not as linear as this time-line. However, in general, to reap the rewards of the process, allow yourself a year without romantic and sexual intrigue. While this may sound like a lot of time now, in the scheme of your life, it's a short amount of time to invest in your-self.

Chapter Eight
Reclaiming Damaged Dreams

Recognizing sexual issues may hurt. But with the pain comes an entry point into the sexual healing journey. When sexual problems surface, they often tell us we have reached a core issue in overall recovery. Once we admit something is wrong, we can direct our energy toward understanding and healing. And healing our sexual concerns can lead us to profound insights about ourselves and to improved relationships with others. The journey has begun.
Wendy Maltz, *The Sexual Healing Journey*[1]

The discussion of trauma in Chapter Six points to the fact that psychological isolation affects the brain. Specifically, survivors endure a loss of functioning in the cognitive processes that involve hoping and dreaming. Healing your addiction means facing the loss of the one dream you had–the fantasy that the perfect relationship will make you whole. As you enter withdrawal from sex and love addiction, you face your greatest fear–being alone. You feel hopeless. You bargain with yourself and others. Maybe there's an easier way. You face times of denial. *I'm not really an addict...I just haven't found the right person.* These are normal responses to the loss of a fantasy and the fear of being alone.

You may recall from earlier chapters that psychological isolation is a terrifying human experience. The fear of being alone is like death. Yet in withdrawal, this is the very fear you're facing. Facing death is a humbling experience. In his book, *Existential Psychotherapy,* Irving Yalom, states the following about death:

Death and life are interdependent: though the physicality of death destroys us, the idea of death saves us. Recognition of death contributes a sense of poignancy to life, provides a radical shift in life perspective, and can transport one from a mode of living characterized by diversions, tranquilization, and petty anxieties to a more authentic mode.[2]

In withdrawal, "diversions and tranquilizations" stop. Your disease no longer anesthetizes you to the reality of your humanity. You stop running from the fact that you're like everyone else. Someday, you will die. You are human, imperfect, vulnerable and, ultimately, beautiful. In *Radical Acceptance,* author Tara Brach, Ph.D., explains,

... times of great suffering can become times of profound spiritual insight and opening...at these times, all the beliefs upon which we based our life are torn from their moorings; we thought we understood how to live life but now we feel lost in a stormy sea. As the storm quiets, we begin to see our life with freshness and a striking clarity.[3]

The process of withdrawal is a time of "great suffering." By entering into a withdrawal period, your negative beliefs "are torn from their moorings" and no longer provide the foundation of your thought process. The belief that no one could love you if they really knew you, or no one can be trusted, cannot survive the "freshness and striking clarity" that comes during withdrawal. Trust in your basic goodness returns. You reclaim the childlike innocence that your *dis-ease* took from you.

One of the greatest thefts of an addiction is the loss of who you really are. In active addiction, it's easy to deny your true purpose in life, your talents, goals, and dreams. Denial permits you a false sense of strength while hiding your true creativity. Withdrawal brings back a chance for you to have a wide range of experiences including joy, pain, pleasure, and intimacy. Recovery allows you to reclaim damaged dreams.

Tools for Transformation

As you shed the darkness of addiction, the gift of yourself is the ultimate reward.

When we see the secret beauty of ourselves, we see.... into the core of who we truly are–not an entrapped self but the radiance of goodness.[4]

In recovery and withdrawal, your energy no longer goes to maintain the addictive cycle. Instead, you're free to excavate your soul. Remember Heather's words: she felt like a sculptor was taking a chisel to her head during early withdrawal. Spiritual transformation doesn't come without pain, and it won't happen in isolation. Professional support and the company of other recovering women are critical for success during withdrawal and recovery from love and sex addiction.

Professional support

When you begin treating this addiction, you'll be healing your brain. You cannot heal your brain alone. The brain doesn't function at full capacity when you feel isolated. Therefore, you need a relationship in which to heal. In *Making a Good Brain Great,* Dr. Daniel Amen shares the results of his research.

Your brain determines your effectiveness in life...When your brain works right, you have full access to your true nature. On the other hand, when your brain is troubled you are more likely to struggle at work, in relationships, within yourself, and in society. When your brain is troubled, you have trouble being your best self and often act outside your own values, morals, and desires.[5]

Women suffering from sex and love addiction are "troubled" and have difficulty being their best selves. Most of their sexual and romantic behavior falls outside their value system. Many times, they don't know their true desires. Healing your life means healing your brain. To do this, you need professional support. Dr. Jean Baker Miller and Dr. Irene Stiver assert that "the centerpiece of therapy is the creation of a new relationship."[6] Not a romantic relationship, but a safe relationship. A trusting relationship gives you a context for healing. Many recovering women find this safe relationship in a therapeutic setting. Choosing the right therapist to accompany you on this healing journey is a valuable step in the right direction. The caregiver is essential for your healing. It's important to keep the following things in mind when you are ready to find a therapist if you don't have one already.

- Be a careful consumer. Not every therapist is the same. You deserve to have the best fit for you. Look for a professional who is open-minded, current on the latest research, and willing to try new things. You will spend time and money in therapy. Make a wise investment and interview a number of professionals until you find the right person for you.

- Some professionals have published articles or books, or speak at local meetings where you can find out more about the work they do.

- Consider finding a professional who understands brain chemistry, the effects of trauma, and the subsequent need for an addiction.

- It can be very helpful if your therapist understands sex and love addiction, and can guide you through the process of designing a treatment plan that will best address your particular situation.

- Most important, your therapist must be able to facilitate a relationship with you that is collaborative and respectful. If you feel awkward in your first meeting, listen to your intuition. Trust your heart to be your guide in finding the right professional.

Group support

Many women recovering from sex and love addiction believe group participation is the key ingredient for their sexual healing process. Addiction literature of all types supports the overwhelming evidence that 12-step groups facilitate recovery from addictions. Although 12-step groups are not the only option for group support, they are one of the best.

However, for many women, attending a 12-step meeting brings a feeling of dread. There are many reasons for this, but one of the biggest is the fact that 12-step programs talk about God. "I don't believe in God" or "those ideas won't work for me" are common responses to the idea of attending a 12-step meeting.

Survivors of childhood abuse commonly have an aversion to God. Since authority figures give us our first idea of God, most children form a God-concept that is like Mom or Dad. If caregivers were abusive, there is no reason to trust a loving Higher Power.

When you have endured spiritual and emotional abuse in your family and/or in a church, references to God or patriarchal theological teachings can be disturbing. Churches and religious traditions become triggers for pain. You may struggle with the male face of God that brings anti-feminine associations or reminders of abuse. As a result, religious trauma becomes a true stumbling block in the recovery from an addiction.

For this reason, a discussion of 12-step programs from a psychological perspective, rather than a theological perspective, can be helpful. Why are these groups successful? What if you don't believe in God? Can they still help? The answer is yes. They can still help. For more information on specifically how and why 12-step groups work, you may refer to the discussion at the back of this chapter.

Gifts of Recovery

To recover means "the getting back of something lost" or "to restore."[7] Healing from an addiction is commonly referred to as recovery. Piece by piece, therapy and the 12-steps help women recover their stolen innocence. Women in recovery talk about finding parts of themselves they thought were lost.

For me, it was the simple things at first...like one summer, two years into recovery, I did a flip off the diving board. I felt euphoric! I was thirty-two years old and felt like I was eight, free and fun and full of life. I thought those feelings were gone forever.

I remember taking a nap one afternoon, and thinking to myself, it's OK. The world will not end if I rest. I learned in recovery that keeping things slow and simple made me feel better. I didn't have to be in a frenzy all the time to prove that I was worth something.

My favorite gift in recovery is learning that I like my own company. What an incredible feeling. Now, it's less of a surprise to me when others want to be with me. It's not perfect. I still have days when I need reassurance from the people I love. But most days, I know I'm loveable and fun.

Diminishing fear

Addiction is a strategy to deal with constant fear. For protection, abuse survivors learn to cultivate an emotional and spiritual dishonesty that ultimately leads to a life of secrets. Overt and covert secrets are a product of the fear that you aren't loveable. The irony is that your hidden life prevents true self-confidence. You may appear strong, invulnerable and put together, but deep down you have a sense that you're a fraud. You fear being discovered for who you really are. Fear tells you that your intuition, your spirit, and your talents are permanently flawed. This type of fear gradually corrodes your life, causing high levels of stress and despair. Fear penetrates the nighttime, quiet moments, or certain endeavors.

Barbara, age fifty-nine, recalls her paralyzing fear of traveling alone. "I cancelled a business trip because I didn't want to travel without my husband. I felt so ashamed." One client, age forty-five, recalls her fear of buying a home.

At work, everyone trusts my instincts and abilities. But when it comes to making an investment in myself, I freeze. I don't trust myself to do it right. I can shop for clothes or shoes without a problem, but when it comes to a grown up purchase like a home, I can't do it...I still feel too young or inept. It's as if I'm faking it all the time, pretending to be a grown woman.

In recovery, you're called to face your fear. In the words of Wayne Muller, therapist, author, and public speaker,

... as we move closer to our fears, as we accept them, explore them, and examine our response to the anticipation of danger, we may begin to discover that we have within ourselves all that is required to feel protected and safe.[8]

Muller's words echo what women find during withdrawal–facing your fear unveils the capacity you have to survive whatever life sends your way. In 12-step circles, this is referred to as learning to live "life on life's terms." Muller explains,

... the more we are present with ourselves in fear, without withdrawing, hiding out, or armoring ourselves, the more trust we develop in our own resources, our own creativity, resilience, and wisdom.[9]

After a couple of years in recovery, Maria recalls the first day she experienced a moment without fear. She was sitting in a 12-step meeting and

... suddenly, my body felt different. I didn't feel tight or anxious. Warmth flooded through me and I felt relaxed. I knew, for the first time, I was a woman and I was safe. And my life was mine. It felt incredible.

Tori remembers a similar experience.

Talking about my story to a therapist one afternoon, I knew I was a recovering woman. I could share about my deepest wounds without the fear that they defined me.

As fear diminishes, women talk of feeling lighter and happier. Some are able to sleep peacefully for the first time. "I learned to enjoy going to sleep," says Jane. "Without constant fear, nighttime became comforting rather than dreadful." Like Jane, many sex and love addicts suffer interrupted sleep due to residual fear. Some resort to medication. But troubled sleep can sometimes indicate deeper issues that need your attention. Facing these issues brings ultimate freedom from fear. When you face your fears, you learn that "somehow, within [yourself], all will be well."[10]

Reducing shame

Daily abstinence from addictive behavior reduces shame. Therapy and group support also heal shame. The belief that "I am basically an unworthy person" diminishes with the right treatment. Jane chuckles as she shares her new comfort with her body.

I couldn't even undress in front of my cat when I was in early recovery. Without my addiction to keep me numb, shame seemed to cover my whole body. It was disgusting. Now, I smile as I get dressed in the morning, and no longer hide from my image in the mirror, or from my cat....it's such a relief.

Shame creates confusion and disorientation. As a result, although you have an adult body, inside you may still feel very young. Youthful feelings are shared among trauma survivors or children who grew up in families where addiction was present. Furthermore, feelings of uniqueness seem to be a product of shame and isolation. Shame leaves you feeling different somehow—an outsider in the human race. Belonging to a group heals this feeling. You learn that others have similar experiences. They share your negative beliefs.

Most addicts believe that "if anyone really knew me, they wouldn't love me." In groups and with the help of professional support, your shame begins to heal and former feelings of confusion dissipate. You feel older, more confident and more serene. According to Sharon Salzberg,

Serenity is the most important ingredient in being able to be present or being able to concentrate the mind. Concentration is an act of cherishing a chosen object. ... When we can concentrate, all of this energy is returned to us.[11]

Reducing shame prepares us for love, to "cherish" another and ourselves.

Transforming Anger

Anger, whether eroticized or not, can be a true feeling of power. Directing anger at someone we believe deserves our wrath temporarily relieves feelings of fear and vulnerability. For example, Brooklyn had trouble feeling pain. When she felt it, she felt weak. In her "bodymind," weakness meant she would be hurt, as she had been in her childhood, so Brooklyn learned to be angry when she was in pain.

She spent much of her energy being angry at her father. She desperately wanted his apology. She wanted him to make right what was done horribly wrong. This is a common and understandable desire.

However, the desire for a parent's apology or admission of guilt can delay necessary healing. It is a way to maintain denial: the denial that as a child you were not protected and cherished. In this way, denial can be gift. It's terribly painful to sit with the truth of being abused. But waiting for closure can sometimes justify behavior that is hurtful to yourself and others. In Brooklyn's case, she continued to act out her anger in her marriage, hurting both herself and her husband.

In Heather's active addiction, she justified her use of men as a way to avoid her feelings for Mark. In truth, her relationship with Mark was a replay of her parents' abandoning love. As long as she stayed connected to him, she kept her feelings of anger and betrayal alive, maintaining her perceived status as an "outsider."

In recovery, Heather faced the anger she felt for her parents. She addressed the pain of being left out in her family. As her anger healed, so did her need to hurt herself and others. Without the burden of anger and resentment, she was able to let go of her obsession with Mark. She opened up for the possibility of authentic intimacy.

Healing Grief

Before the gifts of recovery are truly yours, you must grieve. Recovering from this disease is facing the loss of a fantasy. The fantasy has been your best friend, your greatest comfort, your closest companion for most of your life. Even though the fantasy has become a source of agony, letting it go still hurts. Your dreams are dying, and death brings grief.

When a loved one dies, we are surrounded by concerned friends and family. There is sympathy and concrete support. Even businesses make time for loss with bereavement leave. However, in most cases, we're expected to rebound within weeks. Sadly, our culture doesn't really understand grief. But in the case of recovery, you're facing an even greater cultural misunderstanding. Letting go of this disease gets no cultural support or recognition. You'll have days where you simply cannot imagine working, yet you will be expected to do so. Withdrawal can be the loneliest time in your life. In many cases, you can't explain to family or friends what you're going through. For this reason, it's critical to have a therapist and a group to support you.

You may wonder, what's the point? If recovery hurts so badly, why do it? It's time to remember your goals and who you want to be. It's also important to stay focused on the truth of the loneliness of your disease. As long as you rely on your addiction to bring you energy, power or love, you will lose. Surrendering brings pain, yes, but it's clean pain. The pain of grief is very different from the pain that comes from compulsive behavior. Compulsive behavior keeps unbearable shame in your life. You simply cannot be authentically proud of who you are while you're in your disease. The shame that accompanies addiction feels dirty and heavy, like a sludge you can't remove. But the clean pain of grief has a purpose. It hurts because it's supposed to. Like the pain of childbirth, it makes sense. And it doesn't last.

In the words of M. Scott Peck, "Life is difficult."[12] If we accept this statement, then pain is no one's fault. Part of the human condition is experiencing pain. No one gets by without suffering. By facing pain directly, you find tenderness in yourself. Experiencing your own anger, fear, and grief, you feel the vulnerability in others. Your heart becomes soft and open as you regain the humanity and heart your addiction stole from you. According to Muller,

Once we remove the question "why," we may see our pain face to face, accepting it for what it is. Then we can begin to truly grieve, which softens the pain. The deep hurt and anger and sadness can then lead us to letting go, to forgiveness, and to healing.[13]

Sometimes grief lasts for hours, days, even weeks. Grief feels endless. It's a messy process with no particular rules. Learning to handle grief brings richness to your life that can be reached no other way. It's an avenue to meaning–a path to abundance and joy. Consider the following:

Tori
Each time I grieve, I feel a little lighter, a little more free. As I reclaim lost feelings of sadness, other feelings bubble up as well and I discover a range of emotions that sometimes include humor and happiness. The steps are teaching me to release the past and look forward to the future. They are diminishing my fear.

Maria
When I first began to grieve, it felt like chewing glass. The pain seemed limitless. But each time I survived a wave of grief, I felt cleaned out. I felt fresh. In time, grief became less threatening, and although I still fight it, when I can remind myself to surrender, grief always brings me a closer to myself.

Barbara
One of the gifts of growing older and being in recovery is learning that I'm not in charge of everything. Now, when grief comes my way, I don't fight it. I surrender. I remember one weekend with a friend. We were supposed to be working on a project together. But I woke one morning missing my husband and feeling grief about our marriage. I knew we were supposed to be getting work done, but I also knew myself. I couldn't be productive while grieving. So I gave into it, and shared my feelings with her. She listened, and patiently waited with me for the pain to pass. I didn't have to be alone with it. The next day, I felt happy and soft. I could focus on our work. Grief had run through me. Not only did we accom-

plish our project, but our friendship grew deeper as a result of sharing.

Barbara's words speak to the nature of grief. It teaches us to be humble. We're no longer responsible for living up to the imagined expectations of everyone around us, or the impossible standards we've created for ourselves. Instead, we're free to live each moment listening to the truth in our body, heart, mind, and spirit.

Reclaiming Damaged Dreams

As gray, as controlled, as dreamless as we may strive to be, the fire of our dreams will not stay buried. The embers are always there, stirring in our frozen souls like winter leaves.[14]

In order to live a meaningful life, you must first have the ability to envision what you want. You must be able to dream. In order to do this, you need free choice, self-acceptance, and self-consciousness. You must also learn how to play. For many survivors, the ability to play was lost. Life became much too serious too soon. Addiction has been your only playing field.

Psychotherapy and group support reduces shame and restores your natural ability to hope, dream, and play. The joy of recovery is building the life you want. You reclaim dreams that have been damaged. When you begin recovery and take an inventory of your life, you may not find much that you like about it. You may have alienated or abandoned friends. You may have lost dignity and strength. Your health may be failing. Your life has been built in reaction to the wants and needs of others instead of your own, leaving you angry, depressed, victimized, and confused. You've lost sight of who you want to be.

But with time in recovery, you begin to feel better. You start to like yourself. When you like who you are, you naturally begin to acquire what you need to be happy and enjoy life. You stop waiting for someone else to do it for you. According to Julia Cameron, author of the *Artist's Way*, "Each of us has an inner dream that we can unfold if we will just have the courage to admit what it is."[15]

When you no longer feel guilty or ashamed if something good happens for you, you can find your inner dream. When you begin to know your worth, you can find your inner dream. When you embrace authentic joy and pleasure, you can find your inner dream. This is the reward of recovery.

It's not a perfect process. Sometimes we get confused and instead of asking for physical touch or nurturing, we buy a new car or new clothes. Perhaps we need more spiritual time, but instead we look for more sex. Identifying wants and needs after a lifetime of ignoring them takes time. Ambivalence is our great enemy in recovery. When we are ambivalent about our wants, needs, or sexual desires, the world around us appears scarce rather than abundant, chaotic rather than pleasing, and we can't find our way. We may again start to feel self-pity and wonder why life is so difficult.

But if you remain steadfast to the process of recovery, attend regular therapy appointments, and work the steps in your 12-step meeting, you will find your path. You will find that decision making gets easier and you instinctively know the next right thing to do. Anticipate new ideas about careers, creative pursuits, romantic hopes, and lifestyle changes. Greater satisfaction, serenity, and joy emerge as the ability to identify and meet your healthy desires is restored.

In withdrawal, you have known darkness. It's been messy, murky, and yet somehow necessary. You needed time to be deep inside yourself, back in the womb, hidden and safe from the world. As you emerge from the darkness, however, you have more energy and new focus. You're ready to give birth to your true self. Sometimes, the changes are immediate and concrete. Jane shares how she invested in herself after a year of abstinence from sexual behavior and dating.

I finally took a trip to Europe that I had always dreamed of taking. I quit waiting for someone to make it happen for me.

Other times, the changes are more internal. Tori shares her process.

Recovery brought me to a place of realizing that I had been programmed to want marriage. My mother's focus had always been my father. But the more I learned about myself and healed the pain of my family chaos, I learned that marriage did not really appeal to me. I'm not sure why, but for now, I'm content to have a boyfriend and take each day as it comes. Marriage is not my goal. Staying in recovery is. I'm learning so much about myself every day, and enjoying my work, friends and hobbies. Life is starting to be fun. I never knew it could be like this.

Tori's self-awareness reflects the inner awakening that comes with recovery. Without constant fear, shame, and anger, your true self comes out of the darkness. Like Tori, Heather's changes involved much internal reflection. Her external world changed a great deal as her healing progressed.

After a few years of working the steps and seeing a therapist who understood my addiction, I started to examine my career. At the time I was modeling, and although I was earning a nice amount of money, I felt part of me was being wasted. I had always been a great student, and I missed the challenge of an academic environment. So, with prayer and meditation, my focus each day was on finding the right path for my talents. My therapist encouraged me to keep a journal as this process unfolded. Writing helped me stay clear about my thoughts and my desires. It became impossible to ignore the inner voice inside that kept telling me to follow my dreams.

In a few months, clarity came and I decided to go to law school. I had always wanted to do this. But fear kept me hostage, telling me I'd never be smart enough or good enough. But two years into the rigorous academic program, I felt great–alive and challenged. At times it was difficult and I felt discouraged, but mostly, it seemed I had come home to a part of myself that I had missed dearly.

Cameron explains that "Creativity–like life itself–begins in darkness."[16] Addictive energy is creative energy. When addiction is active all your creative focus goes to maintaining it. When you step away from your disease, after the initial "darkness," your creative energy returns. Creativity is yours to channel in healthy ways. When you apply even a fraction of the creativity it took you to maintain your addiction, the results can be life changing. Consider Maria's words:

Because I had an advanced degree, people around me always thought I had a stimulating career. No one knew the emptiness I felt inside. My addiction had always filled that place in me that needed a creative outlet. Before I started recovery, my friends kind of envied me at times. They thought I was sexually uninhibited, daring, fun, and maybe a bit crazy. But they didn't know I was hiding a restlessness that was about not having my own life. I felt lost, like I would never know the happiness of a fulfilling career or relationship.

Five years into recovery, I hit a sort of limit with my work. It was hard, joyless, and just not me. One of my favorite things to do had always been fixing up my home. So, with the support of my recovery friends, I went back to school to learn interior decorating. This never would have been acceptable in my family of origin. They would have seen it as a waste of talent. But I was in heaven. School was easy for me for the first time in my life. I could actually concentrate!

After I graduated, I began my own business, and in a couple of years, it was flourishing. I woke up every day pinching myself, giddy with the reality of what I was creating. Now when I think of all the time I wasted in my addiction, I feel some sadness. I know it took me the pain of my disease to get where I am now, but it's sad to think of the way I treated myself and others.

The Healing Paradox

There is more shame around sex and love addiction than other addictions. Many individuals who are chemical addicts, food addicts, or even "co-addicts" readily admit they would rather have their addiction than a sex and love addiction. However, the truth is that women recovering from sex and love addiction sometimes get to the core of important life issues faster than other addicts. In the words of addiction specialist Carnes,

Sex seems to be the area of life that most deeply touches our personal issues. Whatever problems we face in life sooner or later impact our sexuality. If we are chronically angry, the anger will eventually becomes sexualized. If we cannot

tolerate closeness, we will fail at sexual intimacy. If we need to be in control, pas-
sion will elude us. If we have experienced trauma, we may repeat it compulsive-
ly through how we express our sexuality. If we are perfectionistic, sexual
response will elude us. And, if we are so overextended and driven that all of our
important relationships are abbreviated, sex will seem brief and overrated.[17]

When you're healing you must truly face the core of who you are. Your sexuality is your center. Sex and the self are intertwined. Paradoxically, treating an
addiction to sex and love leads you to healthy sex and love. Intimacy fear is
under all addictive escape. Addicts in recovery from substances ultimately face
their fear of sex, love, and romance. So when you treat the sexual issues, you go
right to the heart of the matter.

The 12-Step Experience

Children raised in painful families rarely experience a sense of belonging. Many
felt unwelcome in their own homes. You may remember Heather's words–she
felt like an "outsider" in her family. For most addicts, underneath painful behavior is the sense that safety, care, and belonging don't exist. Research shows that
individuals heal this impaired thinking in therapy groups.[18] Group dynamics
facilitate healing in unique ways that determine how and why people get better
when they participate in groups. Although current research is modeled after ther-
apist-led groups, the same principles apply to 12-step programs.

12-Step Groups and Belonging

Families that were psychologically lonely places to grow up have been part of
creating your need for an addiction. You needed a place to hide. Before you had
your addiction, some of you hid in books, in your room, at the neighbor's, in the
garage, or in the life of television characters. You didn't receive the benefits that
come with belonging to a family. They include:

- a sense of belonging
- seeing and being seen
- having your own voice
- supporting others when they have a turn to speak
- giving and receiving comfort when life is painful

In 12-step groups, guidelines serve to protect all group members. Rules about
discussion insure that only one person speaks at a time, no one can dominate the
conversation, and no one is permitted to give advice. Guidelines designed for
anonymity and confidentiality create a feeling of safety while you're in the group.
You can share your voice and listen to others.

Experienced members in 12-step groups have learned how to talk honestly
and openly. They know how to be vulnerable. They've learned it's safe in the
group and necessary for healing. It's an incredible feeling to see someone tell the

truth. In time, the group becomes the safe relationship or family you've needed all along. Twelve-step groups unveil the truth that you're valuable and you have a place of belonging in the human race.

12-Step Groups and Vulnerability

Individuals heal when they are able to explore feelings, vent, and gain relief from expression. Sharing emotions or painful memories in a group allows you to be seen. When others witness your feelings of pain or joy, the experience is transformative. Research shows that having a witness to your life experience is the most curative factor in healing trauma.

Special note: Sharing may sound terrible for you at this point. Shame inhibits any desire to be seen (except perhaps in a sexual way). One woman shared in therapy that it took her an entire year of sitting in 12-step meetings before she would speak to anyone. There is no hurry to be vulnerable in 12-step groups. The pace and the choice are yours.

12-Step Groups and Hope

If you're considering a 12-step group, you have most likely tried other ways to heal without much success. Your negative belief system and impaired thinking get in your way. When a familiar pain is triggered, feelings of hopelessness and despair emerge. You feel stuck. There are neurochemical reasons for this feeling. Helpless feelings born from early childhood fear are lodged in the primal center of your brain which doesn't know time and sequence.

Listening to the stories from others begins to heal your brain by forming connections out of the damaged emotional center into the frontal lobes, creating new pathways for hope. Hope brings inspiration for healing. It's finally because you are no longer alone with your painful thinking. Heather says,

I never felt safe or loved in a church. It always seemed like I had to act a certain way, dress nicely, and present an image in order to be accepted. In recovery, I have felt more hope in 12-step meetings than I ever did in church.

12-Step Groups and Participation

For many abuse survivors, being part of a group effort isn't appealing at first. Either you've learned to avoid groups because you feel different from everyone, trapped by the thought that you must earn your place in the world and nothing you achieve will ever be good enough. Or you typically rise to leadership positions in groups and everyone counts on you to do all the work. Feeling taken advantage of, you may have found yourself disillusioned with group endeavors. Twelve-step groups protect against unhealthy ways of being in groups. No single person leads the group. And no one person handles all the work.

Participation is simple: show up and take a seat. In 12-step groups, you don't have to perform, be perfect, or wear a happy face for others to accept you. It's safe to come out of self-imposed exile. For the hour that you're in a 12-step meeting, you actually begin to whittle away at the paralyzing effects of shame.

12-Step Groups and Relationships

In groups, we learn that life doesn't always unfold as expected. We see how others deal with similar disappointments, tragedies, and loss. From relational learning, we slowly discover our wants and needs and learn to express them. We learn we are OK. Perhaps this is the most powerful form of learning since it comes from relationship. According to Gerald Corey, author of *Theory and Practice of Group Counseling,* the experience of

... empathy, acceptance, caring, and intimacy that develop within a group can be a manifestation of love in the best sense. The intimacy and love that develop among members is often the outcome of the commitment of members to let themselves be known in significant ways, which makes it possible to genuinely love others.[19]

In 12-step groups, you have an opportunity to be with others in non-romantic ways. You learn to listen without taking things personally. In time, you learn to speak without shame, fear, or the expectation of a certain outcome. You learn you are accepted. And acceptance feels like love. Many women find that the experience of unconditional acceptance gives them the first taste of true connection. And this experience crosses gender.

Maria

My first 12-step experience was in SLAA meetings. And the meetings were for both men and women. There were clear guidelines about who to talk to after meetings, emotional intrigue, and flirting. In other words, I was instructed to stick with women. But I got to hear men talk in these rooms. I learned that they had pain just like mine. Without this experience, I don't know how I would have learned that men are human. It was a huge part of my success in recovery and, ultimately, in a romantic relationship. I became tender toward men in a new way...not because I wanted their attention, but because they were just like me.

Jane

When I first started SLAA, I had already been in 12-step recovery for alcohol addiction. I knew that in some groups, men used the time to flirt with women new to a group. Also, it was too easy for me to engage a man in eye contact during a meeting if I was having a bad day and wanted a quick "hit."

In my early AA days, sexual experiences with other group members were all too common, and I was afraid that this would happen in SLAA. So, I started attending a women-only group. I found that I could trust myself better if I had no one to flirt with. It made it easier. Eventually, I noticed that the new boundaries I was learning in SLAA made my participation in AA more rewarding and authen-

tic. *I learned to avoid men who put out sexual signals, and be supportive of the men who were trying to be socially and romantically sober. I learned to have men as friends, and I learned to be a trustworthy woman. This helped women trust me, too. I began to have real friends.*

12-Step Groups and Wisdom

The familiar saying "knowledge is power" aptly applies to addiction groups. In 12-step meetings, part of healing is the acquisition of wisdom. The more you learn about your disease, the more power you have to heal. Education dissolves the mystery of romance addiction, how it works, and why it wins. You learn the signs that indicate fantasy thinking, craving, possible relapse, and new ways your addiction will emerge despite your efforts to stop.

Many women from troubled families didn't have healthy role models. Their parents didn't handle money, conflict, self-care, or nutrition in healthy ways. Twelve-step groups operate on the principle of "attraction not promotion," meaning no one should preach to you about how to behave or what action to take. Rather, you will be given the opportunity to see many different ways people solve their problems, ask questions, and decide for yourself. If someone "attracts" you in a meeting, not in a romantic or sexual way, but in a way that you think "hmmm, I like that person's way of being," then you might wonder how they achieved what they have. It might work for you, too.

This is why members of 12-step programs attend for years. The more seasoned members understand that part of the miracle of recovery is giving back to the group. Service work is simply showing up, taking part in the meeting, and speaking about how it worked for them. Wise members understand that for a newcomer, the group works better if there are long-term recovering individuals in the room.

With 12-step groups, there are no limits to the number of meetings you may attend. There are no financial requirements. And meetings take place daily, sometimes hourly. Since groups reprogram your brain for relationship, attending meetings regularly makes sense. It speeds up the healing process. Shame is reduced faster. Loneliness is eased. Women find that the more often they participate in group meetings, the sooner life calms down. Solutions to previous problems emerge, and chaos dwindles.

12-Step Groups and Authority

Research shows one major weakness for therapy groups–the reality of the therapist. Having a therapist in a group puts an authority figure in the room. For most trauma survivors, authority figures represent trouble. Some women shy away from talking when an authority figure is in the group. Others may try to please the authority figure. Some will express overt or covert anger toward the therapist. Interestingly, 12-step groups protect against this phenomenon; there is no authority person in the room. Twelve-step groups are not therapy groups. It's understood in 12-step groups that the only authority is a Higher Power.

No person takes this role. There is no leader. In this fashion, each person is equal. No one is better than anyone else, regardless of time in the program, gender, sexual orientation, race, socio-economic background, or profession. In fact, guidelines protect members from discussing professional issues for this very reason. In the group, everyone is there for one reason–to heal. Additionally, you're encouraged to choose a sponsor. A sponsor is someone who can take you through the twelve steps and share her experience with you.

In sex and love addiction recovery, the sponsor is critical. She can model healthy ways of being in relationship. By sharing with your sponsor, you learn to ask for help and to be vulnerable. As you progress in your recovery, you develop positive images of yourself as a sexual person. It will be very helpful for you have a sponsor who feels comfortable with herself sexually and who enjoys healthy relationships.

12-Step Groups and Spirituality

When individuals gather for healing purposes, something divine happens. It's risky to trust others and be the new person in a group. However, risk brings vulnerability, which is the first step toward authentic connection with others. You may not believe it's possible that a group could help you. As you consider a 12-step group, you're taking a leap of faith. A spiritual leap takes incredible courage, perhaps a bit of desperation, and true strength of character. As you embark on this journey of self-discovery, cradle your fear in a blanket of knowledge that there is hope.

Chapter Nine
Living Recovery:
Restoring Healthy Relationships

The simple act of being completely present to another person is truly an act of love–no drama is required.
Sharon Salzberg, *Loving Kindness* [1]

Living Recovery: Restoring Healthy Relationships

If you're a true sex and love addict, you may have flipped to this chapter before reading the other ones. Maybe you're hoping that if you read it, you will find out how to have better sex or more intimacy with your current partner. Or perhaps you've been without a lover for a while and you're hoping for a new one. You're not alone. The search for happy relationships and passionate sexuality seems to be universal. Most of us have a craving for something divine that drives our search for meaningful love and sex.

However, if indeed you are addicted to love, sex, or relationships, this chapter may not give you the answers you're looking for. Chapter Nine is designed for those who have fully accepted this disease, entered withdrawal, and surrendered to the process of healing both their cultural inheritance and early childhood wounding.

To enjoy an intimate, romantic relationship, you must become a student of love. It's beyond the scope of this book to explore the many intricacies of healthy romantic love. There are so many wonderful resources for this kind of ongoing study. You will find a resource list at the back of this book to further guide you along the path of discovering all that love can be in an intimate relationship. In this chapter, you will find the seeds with which to grow this kind of bond. In fact, you are planting them now. Simply by identifying your addiction to love and sex, and being willing to treat it, you have already embraced a journey toward love.

As a recovering sex and love addict, you automatically prepare yourself for intimacy by following the treatment plan. If you focus on your goals, attend therapy, and find a group to support your process, you cultivate a field for intimacy. In therapy and through the twelve steps, you learn the following:

You learn to take better care of yourself.
You discover who you are.
You learn to bond with others.

These three important accomplishments set you up for a life beyond your most creative dreams. And they prepare you for healthy sexual relationships. It's like basic training for intimacy. Loving takes practice, but in your addiction, no amount of practice could teach you to love. Since intimacy requires letting someone know you as you know yourself to be, it means you must have some degree of stable identity.[2] In your addiction, you didn't have enough to start with. Your identity–formed by negative cultural inheritances and family abuse–was too fragile for love. Recovery makes you fit for the journey toward healthy intimacy. Recovery prepares you for love.

Self-Care

Nurtured, nourished people who love themselves and care for themselves are the delight of the universe.
Melody Beattie, *Language of Letting Go*[3]

With appreciation for your painful history, you courageously acknowledge the lack of nurturing you received as a child that has left you comfortable in deprivation. In recovery, deprivation is no longer acceptable. As you reclaim your value and worth, deprivation is unveiled as self-abuse rather than noble frugality or self-control.

Letting go of the disappointments and pain of your upbringing, which are the tasks of recovery, teach your "bodymind" to accept abundance. You learn to embrace the care and love that is available to you. In the words of Muller, "We cannot measure abundance by what we accumulate. Abundance is an experience of the heart..."[4]

Manifesting care and love means nurturing yourself. In doing so, you reprogram the negative belief system that you're unworthy of love. But what is nurturing? What is appropriate self-care? You have not seen models for this. You will find teachers in your group. Your therapist can direct you as well. You will learn to distinguish healthy self-care from overindulgence that leads to shame and despair.

To design healthy nurturing activities, consider the following questions. How do you reward yourself after accomplishing a certain task? How do you comfort yourself when you are sad or tired? How do you treat yourself when you are hungry or lonely? Here are some of the comments from recovering women who learned to take care of themselves in recovery.

I always hated taking baths. I resented the time it took from the more important things I thought I should be doing. But my sponsor told me that I needed to soak each night before bed while in the first thirty days of withdrawal. She told me a bath would be like human hug and help with my cravings to call my boyfriend. I did it. And now, when I'm tired, lonely, or feeling particularly deprived, I take a bath and it still amazes me how much better I feel afterward.

My therapist told me I needed to make a dentist appointment. It had been six years since I'd been to a dentist. She helped me understand that this is part of my job to take care of myself.

Before recovery, I thought I knew how to nurture myself. I was great at spending money on new clothes or makeup. But I learned that the way I felt afterward, ashamed and guilty for spending money that I didn't really have, was a form of self-defeat. It wasn't kind to me at all. I was living in regret and living in debt! For me, self-care meant keeping a budget for the first time in my life. I hated it at first. But as I moved forward in recovery, it started to feel good to live within my means. I felt free, which was strange. I was learning that a healthy "no" is not the same as deprivation.

If I start feeling an energy drain–I don't want to get off the couch, don't want to exercise, don't want to do what I need to do to take care of myself. I have probably crossed an internal boundary where I am expecting the guy I am dating to take care of me; I have abdicated my responsibility for myself.

I couldn't afford to go away for treatment, but in the beginning of my recovery, I felt like it would have been a good idea. So, instead, I made my life a treatment center. I started saving my money for therapy, massage, and better food, and I started each morning with a walk.

I started drinking less caffeine and exercising regularly and my body began to feel better.

The following comments are from women healing their sexual and emotional anorexia.

Deprivation showed all over my life–my baggy clothes, my shaggy hair, and general sloppiness. I just didn't take the time to look pretty. Before recovery, I felt there was something admirable in this. Now, I think this was my way of justifying my confusion about being sexual and being a woman.

One of my greatest joys in recovery is learning that I like pretty clothes. I'm also learning to wear makeup. I've had to swallow some pride. Women I previously judged as vain are now my role models. I look at them with admiration as examples of good self-care. My outside is starting to reflect how I feel inside–pretty.

I got my first manicure when I was thirty years old. I felt so nervous, like I was going to be criticized by my mother for indulging myself. But while I was at the salon, there was a mother with her young daughter getting their nails done together. I overheard that it was the little girl's tenth birthday. I couldn't believe it! I felt so many feelings that day–jealous of the little girl and what she was receiving from her mother, sad for the little girl in me that never had those moments with my mom, and happy that I was giving them to myself now.

Self-Acceptance

Can you imagine a state of mind in which there is no bitter, condemning judgment of oneself? The mind no longer sees the world in terms of good and bad, right and wrong, good and evil.

Sharon Salzberg, *Loving Kindness* [5]

Self-acceptance doesn't release you from responsibility for your actions. It releases you from the self-hatred blocking your ability to respond to life with clarity and balance. When self-hatred governs your thinking process, negative thoughts distort your reality. Self-acceptance isn't possible. Before you can accept who you are, you must acknowledge who you are. As outlined in Chapter Eight, you must face fear, anger, grief, and shame. You must also face who you have been in your active addiction.

Making the effort to establish a safe therapeutic relationship, and completing steps four and five allow you to do this. With professional help and group support, your impaired thinking changes. Keep in mind that it has taken years to develop the self-hate and shame you carry. So it takes time to release these toxic emotions and make room for self-acceptance.

Self-awareness is a critical step in this process. You simply cannot accept what you don't know is there. And you can't know certain things about yourself until it's time. Barbara's experience with her first fourth-step inventory speaks to the beginning of self-acceptance that comes through self-awareness.

Writing my fourth step was very painful. I felt ashamed and embarrassed of who I was as a person. I had never looked at myself on paper. With all the therapy I had done, this was the most revealing experience that I'd ever had. When I shared this with my sponsor, she sat and listened to me tell her the terrible things I had done in my life. She never judged me. She didn't condemn me. She just listened. I'd never had an experience of such total acceptance before. It was profound for me.

Barbara's sponsor accepted her when she couldn't accept herself. This allowed Barbara to heal layers of shame and self-hate. Self-acceptance comes slowly in recovery. It comes from repeated acceptance from others. Tori remembers what this acceptance felt like.

In meetings I felt I was not judged as good or bad. All that seemed to be needed from me was my presence. I'm so glad nothing was asked of me, because I truly had nothing to give.

Heather's words show the profound healing work she has done in recovery.

Self-acceptance means I have learned that I will first sexualize most relationships. I have learned to recognize this and to be gentle with myself while I go through this phase with whatever new relationship or situation I'm in–to know that it will pass.

As Heather heals self-hatred and shame, she experiences a self-acceptance that brings new appreciation for her sexuality.

I have learned that my sexuality is a phenomenal gift–both to myself and my partner. I am not always comfortable with my sexuality but when I can get to a place of acceptance, then I am incredibly grateful, gleefully delighted, and slightly impressed with my sexual warmth and generosity for my partner.

Self-acceptance brings serenity. Rather than being locked in obsession, the mind settles and is free to know what to do. Maria shares how

... when I first heard the word serenity, I wasn't impressed. I didn't think I wanted serenity. It sounded boring. I equated it with a walking death.

After years in recovery, however, Maria's ideas about serenity have changed.

I depended on the intensity of my addiction to feel alive and keep my painful feelings repressed. But after years of healing, peace now brings me joy. It's a glorious pleasure. When I see chaos now, I feel like I'm getting physically ill...it's just not attractive. I find pleasure in my life from moments of stillness and quiet. From a serene place, I most enjoy being sexual with my partner. I no longer need alcohol to be sexual. And I don't need to be stimulated with erotic images.

Awareness does not settle everything. Acceptance doesn't mean you pretend that you're always happy about your life. It means you learn to accept reality, including your human feelings of loss, frustration, and imperfection. Jane explains acceptance in the following way:

Practicing acceptance means I have worked my way through the fact that both my parents were alcoholics, they neglected me, they abused my older brother, who then turned around and abused me physically and sexually. But it also means that the sun may not shine when I want it to, or my dog barks when I need to sleep, and my best friend has cancer. Life hurts sometimes.

Heather says that

... I can accept that life is like a river, moving on whether I agree to it or not. I

can choose to ride the river as it flows or paddle upstream, wearing myself out
on the journey.

Self-acceptance means you embrace your strengths, but also acknowledge and respect your limitations. You learn who you are and who you're not. As judgment and perfectionism heal, you develop compassion for yourself. Because you have accepted the darkness of your addiction, it ceases to run your life. The need for secrets diminishes. You soften toward yourself and become tender toward others. When your behavior and thoughts are free of shame, you live with integrity, taking delight in your actions. Without shame, you become intimate with yourself. In this way, self-acceptance is the foundation for love.

Self-Love

Our self-loathing will always meet us down the road, no matter how fast we run
and what fancy footwork we're doing.[6]

Most women addicted to love and sex struggle with self-hatred inherited from the cultural double bind. By taking on the treatment of sex and love addiction, you face the following task: learning to like being a woman. Part of enjoying healthy relationships is first enjoying you. It's not a cliché. You must love yourself, have compassion for your imperfections, and rejoice in your humanity to extend healthy love to another person. If you are unhappy when you're alone, you will be unsatisfied in a romantic relationship. Do you like your own company? What do you do when you have free time to enjoy yourself? Have you learned to be gentle with yourself when you make a mistake? Do you have compassion for your suffering and pain?

In *Radical Acceptance*, Brach says compassion begins "with being aware of our own pain because once our hearts are tender and open to our own suffering, we can more easily extend compassion to others."[7] Compassion allows you to wish that someone be free from pain. This is a foreign concept for women in addictive relationships. For most sex and love addicts, the experience of wishing the best for someone else has never happened.

You may have pretended to want happiness for someone you love, in an effort to appear worthy of love and attention. But without true compassion for yourself, you haven't been able to extend unconditional goodness to others–even in friendships with women. Part of learning to love yourself is healing your fractured friendships with women and identifying the motives behind your relational gestures. Part of loving you is accepting and cherishing the women in your life.

Women as Friends

According to author and psychologist Brenda Hunter, "Friendship is one of the things women do best. We are better at making friends than many of the things we put our minds to because it comes naturally."[8] Hunter's words are true for many women, however, not for most sex and love addicts. Sex and love addicts generally don't have female friends. Sadly, for most sex and love addicts, other women are competitors. In Jane's words,

I was always sizing up other women to see if they were thinner, prettier, or sexier than me. If they were, I stayed away from them. I couldn't be friends with women unless I felt superior to them.

Barbara talks about women differently than Jane, but feels some similar disconnection from women.

Before recovery, I seemed to attract women who were controlling or bossy, or women I could control and manipulate. There never seemed to be mutuality to my friendships with women...and they were never as important to me as men. In fact, usually, they weren't even on my radar.

For most sex and love addicts, friends fall into the following three categories:

Acting-out friend: the woman you call to accompany you on a hunt (the search for a new partner or a one-night stand). You count on her because she's witty, reckless, and fun-loving. She usually won't judge you for what you are about to do because she's been there, too. However, if her addiction is stronger than yours, you can't be sure she'll be available for you and you may have to resort to a sideline friend.

The sideline friend: women who seem to need your presence to enjoy themselves. They typically bore you, but you will spend time with them because they make you feel important.

The crush: the woman you think you're in love with and hope will feel just as intensely for you. To fill the emptiness inside, you develop a crush on this friend and place unrealistic expectations on the relationship. You may become smothering, controlling, or demanding and drain the life out of the friendship, ultimately chasing her away. Unconscious of how this happens, you repeatedly feel abandoned and betrayed.

At some point in the withdrawal period, faced with restrictions around romantic relationships, you may realize that you have alienated your "friends" with your romantic behavior or your demands for connection. You see that your romantic relationships are not the only broken relationships in your life. Friends have withdrawn from you. Some have scorned you. You have abandoned friends in pursuit of your addiction. Women are a painful reflection of your own self-hatred.

In your addiction, female friendships have been twisted like the longing for sexual intimacy. The loss of female companionship is one of the greatest pains of love and sex addiction. Reclaiming yourself includes building healthy relationships with women. You must learn to have friends. Your ability to integrate women into your life is a measure of your own self-love.

Mother Hunger

The loss of the daughter to the mother, the mother to the daughter, is the essential female tragedy.

Adrienne Rich, *Of Woman Born*[9]

Love and sex addiction is a perversion of the healthy need for human love and connection. It begins early in life. This addiction involves the core of your soul. From the center of your heart, you are afraid of closeness. You have learned to protect yourself from pain and cut yourself off from human intimacy. To heal this fracture, you must begin with the original wound. Culturally, emphasis has been placed on mothers and sons/fathers and daughters. In patriarchal structures, mothers and daughters are overlooked. However, the bond between a mother and her daughter sets up the relational template for a child. It is within this first relationship that a young girl learns to love or to fear, to trust or to hide, to laugh or to cry.

By opening a discussion of mothers and daughters, I want to first explain that this is not an attempt to blame mothers. Mothers are women. As women, mothers inherit the same painful cultural beliefs that their daughters do. Many times, they are also victims of abuse. The following exploration of mother hunger develops with the premise that mothers are first women and, therefore, the pain they inadvertently pass on to their daughters they often endured themselves.

Our mothers are our first love. We are born designed for her embrace. At her breast, we learn the world is either safe and warm or cruel and rejecting. In our first relationship with mother, we begin to form a concept of self. In the words of Hunter, "By using our mother as a mirror, we know what it is to be female."[10]

Sex and love addicted women learn how to be female from their mothers, and the lessons are painful. Women in recovery from sex and love addiction describe their mothers as "rejecting, unpredictable and/or unavailable." Barbara recalls a painful image of her mother that she revealed in therapy. "I could see her clearly…pushing me away from her…handing me over to my dad. She sacrificed me to keep him happy."

As a result of emotional, physical, or sexual abuse, daughters formed either anxious attachment or anxious-avoidant relationships with their mothers. Anxiously attached daughters are clingy and angry in adult relationships. Remember how Maria alienated intimate partners with her intense mood swings and flirtatious behavior? Maria explains,

I could never relax around my mother…it's as if I was waiting for the next critical thing she would say about me. But at the same time, I desperately tried to avoid her scorn by doing or saying things that might please her.

In therapy, Maria learned that she could never please her mother. And that her attempts to do so were harming her. Her efforts to please her mother kept the belief alive that she was somehow unworthy of love.

Daughters who are anxious-avoidant will appear very independent as adults. For these women, their mothers seem insignificant. They have no strong feeling about her one way or another. According to author Adrienne Rich, "the 'mother-less' woman may react by denying her own vulnerability… and the absence of mothering."[11] Barbara's distant relationship with her mother is a good example of an avoidant attachment. When she talks about her mother, Barbara feels nothing.

I don't think my mom liked being a woman. She wasn't nice and she never relaxed or seemed happy, and I think she drank a lot to make her life more bearable.

When Barbara speaks about her mother's death, it's with an absence of emotion. "When my mother died, I felt nothing. Although it's been a few years, I still feel nothing. This makes me sad. I wish I felt something."

Healing the pain of being "unmothered" is sometimes impossible to do with your mother. She may no longer be alive. Perhaps she is consumed in her own addiction and unsafe for you. She may be unable to examine her unhealthy behavior and to share your pain with her would be too risky. Many women face the reality that the emptiness mother left behind will always be there. However, much can be done to soothe the wound. Although it cannot be done with Mom, you can heal with the healthy women you meet in recovery.

Hungry for Love

Expect complications as you develop friendships with women in recovery. You will make mistakes as you try to heal the wounded place in your heart that experienced pain attaching to your mother. This wound is primal. It is old, and it is tender. Many times, it's unrecognizable. But it has set the template for how you relate to others. Growing up separate and alone, we long to be held like children, even as adults. We crave the compassionate heart of an all-loving mother or a merciful father. In addictive relationships, we struggle to have this craving satiated. We place impossible, unconscious expectations on one person to fill all our needs and heal our wounds–even the ones we don't know we have. When he or she inevitably fails, we feel betrayed, confused, and angry.

If you never knew the love of your mother, you carry a profound wound. Your first love failed. As an adult, rejection is at the core of your attachment desires. The need for connection will bring horrible feelings of fear, sadness, rage, or shame that are stored in your "bodymind." In her book *Of Women Born*, Rich says,

The woman who has felt 'unmothered' may seek mothers all her life–may even seek them in men. Some… marry looking for a mother."[12]

Mother hunger is the core of your addiction to love and sex. When you decide you want a healthy loving relationship, you must heal this pain. Until you do, you may experience:

- attracting friends with destructive tendencies like your mother
- rejecting friends who unconsciously remind you of your mother
- committing to men who are your mother's twin
- confusing mother hunger and sexual orientation

Heather

I never felt my mother loved me after she married my stepfather. I was so young, that for most of my life, I felt she had left me. I felt replaced. In my relationships with women as an adult, I repeatedly attract women who leave me. I don't have long-term friendships. This brings me a great deal of shame and pain. I feel deep inside that something is wrong with me. Although I am healing this belief in recovery, relationships with women continue to be challenging for me.

Accepting the love of women, and extending love to women, is an expression of the degree to which you love yourself. Friendship is a reflection of your ability to accept who you are. You must learn how to be a friend and how to accept friendship. A support group is ideal for this kind of learning to take place. The women in your support group can comfort you when you're hurt. They can celebrate your successes. You may never have known this kind of love and acceptance from a woman, and it's time. Repeatedly, women in 12-step recovery say that "the group was my first taste of unconditional love."

Paradoxically, until you can enjoy a healthy bond with a friend, free of romantic or sexual intrigue, you're not available for romantic intimacy. You need friendships before you can embark on a romantic relationship. Without friends, you will always be at risk for addictively acting out. The group teaches you to love yourself by doing it for you when you can't. Loving yourself means re-mothering yourself. This will seem foreign at first. Use your self-care techniques and be with women in your 12-step group. Eventually, you will learn to identify and respect your needs. You will stop rejecting yourself the way you were first rejected. And you will learn to love.

Reflections on Friendship

Tori makes an important observation about friendships. "How can I expect to hang in there with a romantic partner if I've had no practice with commitment in my female friendships?" Jane, previously threatened by beautiful women, comments that

... after a few years in recovery, things changed. I started enjoying all kinds of women, even beautiful women. My friends became an extension of me. As I trust-

ed my own beauty and how to contain it, I trusted that other women could, too. Jane's experience highlights the importance of self-trust. As she learned to have boundaries, contain her sexual energy, and trust her romantic choices, she extended the trust to other women. She felt less suspicious. She could relax and have friends.

Maria discusses how sad it was when she realized how important her friends were to her.

I felt lonely at first. My recovery taught me to value the women in my life, but they all seemed too busy or distracted for me. I had to make new friends. This was a hard, painful process. It was challenging to reach out to women I didn't know and risk being vulnerable. But deep inside, I knew I couldn't expect my pre-recovery friends to be available to me anymore.

Heather's experience, like Maria's, reflects the absence of women friends in her life.

When I first got into therapy years ago, all my friends were guys. I didn't have close female friends, although I had a few "poster" friends that I could trot out from my high school or college days but they never really knew me. It has been a challenge to trust a woman. I have picked more women than I care to count who have "left me" in friendships. I am not certain I believe there will ever be a woman who stays for me as a friend; I don't yet have the capacity to visualize that. However, I do have a glimmer of hope that it is possible.

Recovery and Romantic Relationships

The point of love is to make us grow, not to make us immediately happy.[13]

The miracle of recovery is the discovery of a shared dream–we all want to be happy. The common desire for happiness unites us with others. We recognize the beauty of our common urge and the similarity brings connection. As we witness our pain and hopes in others, we stop being judgmental. There is nothing to judge. We're all the same. In a shared mission with others, we develop the personality structure to love without judgment. In this way, the first threads of intimacy weave their way into our relationships.

According to author Marianne Williamson, "the purpose of intimacy is healing."[14] This may not sound very romantic to you. You may have been hoping for something more intense or exotic. It may be difficult to imagine that healing can coexist with passion and sex. But as you take steps to face your addiction, you have already encountered moments of genuine delight.

Perhaps you are already experiencing the pleasure that comes with self-acceptance. Or the joy of caring for others as opposed to taking care of others. As you have moments of peace or happiness, you may be experiencing the excitement of your own company. If so, you are setting the stage for intimate relationships.

This doesn't mean relationships will be without incredible challenges, times of pain, and periods of darkness. But you have been in the darkness. You have survived it. You no longer need to avoid life in an effort to feel safe. You have a new safety within yourself, and a trust in your ability to handle pain. Through pain and suffering, you are finding authentic strength of character. You are developing the personality structure for love.

The adventure of intimacy requires that you have a self to share. In *Open Hearts,* the authors state that intimacy means the mutual and honest expression of all parts of one's life: anger, worry, elation, sorrow, and other emotions, as well as one's aspirations, dreams, and doubts.[15] In your disease, fear kept you silent. You withheld feelings in an attempt to keep your partner's approval. You hid the parts of yourself you thought were unattractive.

Fortunately, in recovery you come out from hiding. You learn to integrate your darkness and your light. Self-acceptance prepares you for honesty, which is the foundation for intimacy. It's impossible to be honest when you are filled with fear. Fear requires secrets, avoidance, and walls. As fear diminishes, you take down the walls and learn to be honest with yourself and others. Honesty brings vulnerability. Part of becoming fit for love is becoming emotionally ready for vulnerability. In *The Struggle for Intimacy*, author Janet Geringer Woititz explains that

... if you are too terrified of being vulnerable and its consequences to take a risk, you are automatically saying that you are incapable or unwilling to have a healthy relationship[16]

In recovery, you have worked hard to know who you are, accept both your strengths and your weaknesses, and experience a wide range of human feelings. This is both wonderful and terrible. Not all of your feelings are pleasant or mild. You won't always know what to do with them. In this way, a close relationship takes you to another level of self-awareness. In a romantic relationship, you encounter the deepest parts of your heart. As you feel passion and pleasure, you will also find pockets of unhealed fear, anger, and shame. For a recovering sex and love addict, bonding with another person is the most challenging spiritual process you may encounter. You are being called to identify when the urge for closeness is part of your need for a "hit" or a valid need for connection. You are being stretched to know your motives and trust your ability to tell the truth. You are being asked to consider the needs of another person while you are learning to value your own.

It's for these reasons that author David Schnarch says, "Intimacy is not for the faint of heart."[17] When you take on the task of intimacy, you must be willing to work harder at self-care. Rely on the support of your therapist and support group. You can no longer expect romance to meet all your needs.

146

How do I know when I'm ready for a romantic relationship?
The heart becomes supple, or love cannot find us.
Marianne Williamson, *Enchanted Love*[18]

Through the hard work of accepting this addiction, entering withdrawal, and navigating through the healing process, you are becoming prepared for love. Behind walls, you cannot reach out to another person. You stay miserly and guarded with your heart. But in recovery, your walls come down. You become human; fragile and vulnerable, wonderful, and innocent. As you become better at being human, you become better suited for romance.

It is ironic that you must become soft and tender before you take on the challenge of romantic love. The irony is that in weakness comes strength. In brokenness comes humility. And with humility comes a recognition that love is not about getting what you want. It's not about meeting all your needs through one other person. It's a call to cherish and honor someone as you have learned to cherish and honor yourself.

Charlotte Kasl explains that

... without self-awareness, a strong support system, and a sense of personal responsibility, a person is far more susceptible to addictive sexual relationships.[19]

Kasl looks for four things to help her determine if a woman is ready for the challenge of intimacy.

- How much is that person committed to living her own life according to her inner truths?
- Does she see herself as responsible for supporting herself financially?
- Does she create excitement and passion from things she does for herself?
- What is her level of involvement with a support system?[20]

Some of you may be returning to former partners for reconciliation. Some of you will be starting with new partners. Either way, you will need to consider how to measure your readiness. When will you know it's time to explore a romantic relationship? Who will be part of this process with you? Do you have a sponsor or therapist you can trust? One way to determine your readiness is to notice when the question feels less urgent. An urgent need for romance can be a sign that there is still more healing to do. When you have a healthy respect for the task of loving someone, and you feel a sense of awe, you may be ready.

Maria
When I met the person I'm now married to, I had reached a point where, for the first time in my life, I was truly humbled by the idea of love. It was different than the fear of rejection or abandonment I had known in my active addiction. It was

an honest fear of losing me or harming another person. I was afraid I wouldn't be able to hold onto the moments of joy and serenity that I was finding in my life. Before recovery, I could jump into a relationship without thinking. Now, it felt risky. I finally had something to lose and I had a more honest awareness of my sexual power.

Dating Again

Women in recovery need concrete direction when it comes to starting romantic relationships. They want to know how to go about the process without jeopardizing hard earned serenity. Dating presents a very real dilemma in recovery. What is healthy dating? How does it look? Is it fun? Before recovery, dating experiences sounded like this:

Barbara

I don't really "date"...I take hostages. I want someone to move in with me. I can't stand being alone so I am never without a lover.

Tori

I always had sex right away, before I knew anyone, and whether or not it was actually a date. I don't think I even knew what a date was.

Brooklyn

I thought dating was having sex.

Jane

I gave up on dating and sold sex instead. It was easier, but I couldn't reconcile being a prostitute for the rest of my life. As much as it felt like "me," it didn't really. I couldn't talk about my work with the people I cared about. It's not like I could go to them and say, "hey! I got a raise at work..." I got so tired of living a double life.

Maria

If a guy bought something for me, or got aroused in my presence, I felt obligated to have sex with him. So I didn't like dating. I never knew it could be enjoyable. Since I didn't have enough internal resources to say no, I was always on guard and defensive.

Dating takes on new meaning in recovery from romance addiction. It's no longer acceptable to use your body as a commodity. Sex isn't a part of early dating. Frequently, women ask questions about healthy dating before it's time. Eagerness is understandable. But when you are ready to date, you feel less eager about it. You have some healthy fear that comes from knowing you can no longer rely on sexuality as a means of connection early on.

Sexual intimacy evolves from trust, commitment, compassion, and mutual desire. These attributes take time to grow in a relationship. It may be awhile before you trust yourself to wait for a healthy relational foundation before using sex to connect with someone.

Heather learned in recovery that "I must talk about sex with the person I am dating before we actually have sex." She learned that if she wasn't comfortable bringing sex into a discussion, it clearly wasn't time to become sexual. In recovery, it is no longer acceptable for sex to be a substitute for genuine connection.

Barbara met her current husband Brad while they were both in recovery. Brad had been in AA and Barbara in OA and SLAA. Since they both had been married twice, and they were timid about dating. They shared the twelve steps, however, and dated with the assistance of their sponsors and recovery friends. Barbara says, "We both had friends who confronted us gently when we were in denial, or making choices that seemed to put us in jeopardy."

The support of friends you trust is so important when you begin dating. Dating will put you in contact with your drug of choice. It will be risky. You will not always know which direction to go. If you try to proceed in isolation, most likely, your addictive thinking will take over and you may find yourself drowning in old habits. Barbara explains,

We made some mistakes early on, but they didn't unravel us. We had a place to go for advice, suggestions, comfort, and encouragement. Brad would go to a meeting and come back to me with new insight. I would talk to my sponsor and be able to apologize to him for something I did that caused him pain or confusion.

Heather had a wonderful sponsor when it came time for her to begin dating. Her sponsor gave clear guidelines for her to follow that she shared with me:

1. Only one date per week for the first two to three months.
2. A date has a start time and a finish time, it's not an overnight.
3. Conversations include topics that avoid getting too personal for the first six weeks, at least.
4. Remind yourself constantly: "Do I like him?" as opposed to "Does he like me."
5. A person whose sexuality immediately hits you in the gut with a visceral reaction of wanting sex is a person you need to run, not walk away from.
6. Avoid time in either person's home; stay in public spaces.
7. Limit phone time or emailing: Use it to coordinate places and times to meet rather than delve into personal topics.

Heather's perfectionism created difficulty for her as she began dating. She had a tendency to be hard on herself if she made mistakes. Her sponsor encouraged her each step of the way, however, and when the inevitable mistakes happened, Heather could share and learn from them. With the care and compassion of her sponsor, she didn't have to make sense of things in isolation.

I could never do this with my mother. It always had to be "right" and so I just hid my real self. I experienced so much pain that might have been avoided if I had been able to turn to her.

Maria reflects on dating Graham.

Graham asked me out when I was in a withdrawal period. It was painful to tell him "no" because I thought he was so attractive. But I knew if I broke my abstinence period, I would feel terrible. I knew if I went out with him under those conditions, my shame would have taken over and it wouldn't have worked out very well. I tried to explain this to Graham on the phone, but really, what could I say? I didn't know him well enough to go into detail. Luckily, he didn't seem to want much of an explanation. He just seemed to want to get off the phone. Two years after my withdrawal period, I ran into him in the neighborhood, and we started talking. He was timid with me so I took the initiative to ask him out for coffee. He agreed. I was thrilled.

After our first date, I was surprised to find that I felt no particular urge to invite him into my home or go to his. In fact, I didn't even wonder if he would call me.

But Graham did call, and Maria wanted to see him again. They dated slowly. Maria didn't want to involve Graham in her son's life too soon, so she agreed to see him every other week when her son was with his father.

I didn't have guidelines. These ideas were coming to me naturally. It's all I wanted. My life was so full I didn't have much time for a new romance, and it felt healthy.

After a few months, Maria knew she was ready to commit more time and energy to Graham, and the feeling was mutual. Things got difficult, however, six months into the relationship when Graham mentioned the idea of marriage. Inside, Maria panicked. She didn't feel ready for this kind of discussion, yet she knew she really cared for Graham.

I started putting on weight for the first time in years. I felt confused, disoriented, and lost. My body was in such fear that I even skipped a period. My doctor thought I was pregnant, even though I assured her I was not having intercourse. I consulted a nutritionist and started going to more meetings. In therapy, we worked to examine what was creating the fear. It was a terrible time. I remember wanting to hide from the world.

But she didn't. Maria continued to persevere through the fear, and in a few months, she returned to her normal weight. "I still wonder what that was all about. I think it was my body's way of telling me to slow down." She told Graham she was afraid, and they didn't discuss marriage again for another six months. At that time, it had been a year, and Maria knew she was ready to commit to Graham.

Loving in Sobriety

Love is about action and choice. When you have chosen to love someone, you have the responsibility to show your love, not just feel it. This is very difficult for a sex and love addict. Most have learned "if I don't care or want you too much, then it won't hurt when you reject me." When you decide to commit to someone, each day you must intervene on this thinking and risk wanting your partner, and caring for him or her. Wanting will make you vulnerable. But if you can't risk being vulnerable, you aren't ready for love. Love in sobriety unites your ability to think and to feel. It takes an act of will and requires practice. It demands your personal growth.

It is the choice to expend energy in an effort to benefit the other person, knowing that if his or her life is enriched by your effort, you too will find a sense of satisfaction–the satisfaction of having genuinely loved another.[21]

Maria

When I decided to be with Graham exclusively, I was overcome with vulnerability. It came from knowing that he could hurt me. He mattered to me. I was letting him matter.

Maria is thoughtful as she remembers the next step she took with Graham.

I asked him to join me in an RCA meeting. His willingness to do this touched me. I could see that it was a stretch for him; he had never been to a 12-step meeting. He learned a great deal in the meeting and wanted to continue. We dated in the safety of other couples who could guide us. We also started couples therapy as we began to consider marriage.

Maria learned to listen to her intuition in recovery. She knew that loving Graham would bring out her fears and she wanted them to have help with the process.

I didn't want to use my old coping mechanisms...my first concern was to be true to my word and not cause harm to either of us knowingly.

Heather shares about loving and action.

When I learned that my husband felt loved when I gave him some space, at first

I was hurt. Why didn't he want to be with me all the time? But I realized that by giving him what he needed, I was "seeing" him and cherishing him. I felt like a better person by responding to his need for separation.

It also helped me. I found that I could go meet a friend or work out while he had time to himself. Respecting his boundaries helped keep me sober!

Similar to Heather, Tori finds that when she takes care of her needs, her relationship thrives.

I've been with the same man for five years now and I am still surprised how simple it can be. If I'm tired, I take a break. If I'm lonely, I call a friend. I don't have to rely on him for everything. And I feel so much better when I don't. When I do what I need to take care of me, it takes care of the relationship.

Maria smiles when she remembers Graham's first reaction to her need for space. He couldn't understand. But he came to her later and said how much he appreciated her.

He had always felt suffocated by other women. He found ways to escape from them, which usually involved drinking or working too much. With me, he experienced relief that I could take care of myself and he learned that I could handle it when he needed his own time. It's not always smooth...sometimes we each get our feelings hurt. But each time we weather a difference in needs, we come out stronger.

Sexuality
Togetherness has to do with focused attention [22]

When you make the choice to love someone, and you focus on that person, you will naturally want to connect in a physical way with him or her. Sexuality reflects the natural unfolding of intimacy. If you have taken the necessary steps to achieve sexual and emotional sobriety, you are ready to trust your sexual instincts. It won't be perfect. It's risky when you surrender to a sexual expression of who you are. It's helpful to remember a few things when you are ready to share yourself sexually.

Sexual desire is your friend: treating sexual desire as an enemy is no longer acceptable. The need for sexual connection is healthy, and you have worked hard to learn how to integrate sexuality into your life.

Heather
It's difficult to ask for what I want sexually. First, I have to trust that it's OK to want what I want, and then, I have to have the courage to ask my partner for it. Wow, that sure feels exposed. It is still hard for me to talk about my feelings.

152

Maria

I learned sex was "bad" growing up. Initiating sex is hard for me. Deep inside, I feel it's a man's job. But in recovery, I am learning that part of my responsibility as a partner is to take initiative and show desire for my partner. I'm getting better at it, but it still requires an active decision...it's not an impulse that comes naturally.

Barbara

It's difficult for me to be affectionate. Brad feels much better when I stroke him and affirm him with touch. I have to make the effort. Usually, I feel like if we are sexual, it should be enough. But that's my addict thinking.

Sexual desire tells you the truth: If you find yourself shutting down sexually, perhaps your body is trying to get your attention. Are you afraid? Are you getting your needs met or only meeting the needs of your partner? Do you need more support around sexual abuse issues that are emerging?

Barbara and Brad have been married seventeen years. At one point in their marriage, she experienced a time of sexual anorexia that lasted for quite some time. At first, Brad allowed the situation, but in time, as he worked his program, he gently confronted Barbara about his sexual needs that were not being met. Barbara knew this took a lot for Brad to do. So, she listened and did not get defensive or make excuses. She started to address the reason she didn't feel sexual anymore. And by doing so, she uncovered the covert incest with her father and the profound disconnection with her mother. She was able to discuss her new insights with Brad who felt relief that it wasn't his fault.

Sharing my pain with Brad helped. He knew my father was important to me, but had never really understood the full extent of the relationship because neither did I. On some level, I was still Daddy's girl. I had to let go of Daddy to love Brad. I also had to face the fact that I never bonded to my mother. My therapist helped me see that without a bond with her, I had not developed a trust of connection. I was still avoiding closeness out of fear of rejection which made sexual intimacy almost intolerable.

Sexual desire indicates relational issues: If you are craving more touch or attention than you are receiving, what's going on? Rather than act out this desire with a sexual secret, can you share your feelings with your partner? If he or she is responsive, you know you are in a relationship where there is room to heal. Perhaps your partner can't quite understand or help, but if there is a willingness to try, you can find extra support from a professional. You may be able to work it out with the help of a couples sponsor. The important thing is that you both address a sexual issue if there is one.

If, however, your partner has no desire to listen to you or understand your pain, you have a different issue to deal with. Choosing to love someone who cannot accompany you when difficult issues emerge is a form of deprivation.

Tori

Today, I face my difficulties with intimacy. I feel vulnerable and sometimes afraid as I lower the walls that protected me from the pain of my childhood. Before SLAA, I thought intimacy and sex were the same thing. Now I know the difference.

Maria

When Graham and I were first married, I was so excited to be sexual with him. He was a man I actually chose! And I found him wildly attractive. But many times, he didn't seem interested. At first, I tried not to take it personally. But after a few months, I knew something wasn't right. It was starting to feel like anorexia to me. So I told him how much I desired him and felt drawn to him. I explained that by loving him each day, I felt open and tender and wanted to connect physically. At first, he tried to avoid the topic. He said he was just tired. But I knew better. I had come too far to ignore my desire or shame myself for having it. I had to take a stand. It was so hard but I told him that I needed him to explore this issue in therapy. To my surprise and delight, he did.

He uncovered the relationship with his mother that had kept him hostage for so many years. Sex was terrifying for him because it meant he would be engulfed. He was scared! This was amazing for him to see, and wonderfully validating for me. He needed to trust that I could be sexual with him and he would still be safe. By holding onto my desire and confronting him, he was able to uncover important issues in his life. Today our sexual life is alive and blossoming. We are careful with each other and playful.

Maria managed to hold on to her reality even though she risked making her partner angry or sad. This takes incredible strength. Without her recovery, she would not have been able to do this. She would have given in to her partner's wishes, or acted out sexually to feel strong enough to handle the intimacy. In this way, Maria demonstrated her readiness for love and commitment. "Long-term intimacy within marriage hinges on validating yourself rather than 'trusting' your partner to make you feel safe."[23]

For most sex and love addicts, bottom-line behavior around sexuality contains some measure of commitment. Commitment requires a decision to reserve your sexual energy for your partner. How can you trust your ability to do this when you have failed previously?

Keep in mind that being faithful to someone else begins with being faithful to yourself. When you are true to yourself, you make decisions based on what you truly desire and need. You no longer make decisions based on what looks good, or what you think someone else wants you to do. When you follow your own desires and truths, you no longer betray yourself, and it becomes unlikely that you will betray someone you chose to love.

Do you truly desire your partner? Do you feel that this is a relationship worth your energy and time? If you have answered yes, you can trust your choice and your sexual desire will follow.

Think about it: if sexual intimacy has to do with disclosing yourself through sex, people who can let themselves be known have more potential for profound sexual experiences.[24]

If you are being honest with yourself and your partner, sexual desire stays alive. When you start to hide or withdraw, sex will follow. It will become boring and routine. In this way, sexuality is your friend and guide. Pay attention to it as you journey along the path of intimacy.

Conflict

Only when two people have shown each other the worst side of our natures are we truly ready for the task of love.
Marianne Williamson, *Illuminata*[25]

In any healthy relationship, conflict will happen. One popular unhealthy belief about love is that happy couples don't fight. "Love means never having to say you're sorry" is a famous line from the movie *Love Story*. When I hear couples say "we never argue," I don't consider this positive. Conflict comes from anger, and anger contains passion. When you passionately care for someone, you will get angry. If you're never angry, where is the passion? Woititz explains

If you love someone and wish to be intimate with them, you have to be prepared to fight with them. Fighting is one of the most positive forms of intimacy, and anger is one of the most significant relationship gifts. To fight confidently with your partner states that you value and respect your partner as an adult who can handle it. To avoid conflict diminishes your partner, leaving issues unresolved constricting all feelings, including joy, tenderness, and care.[26]

Unresolved issues also kill sexual desire. Therefore, an absence of sexual chemistry may indicate hidden anger. If you pay attention to sexuality along the path to intimacy, you may discover pieces of yourself that need to be exposed and shared in order to enjoy the abundance of intimacy.

In addictive relationships, it isn't safe to express anger because someone is always to blame. In fact, most individual 12-step programs warn against anger. *Alcoholics Anonymous - Big Book* clearly says that anger is no longer the privilege of an addict.[27] Truthfully, active addicts cannot manage anger in healthy ways, so the *Big Book* offers wisdom. But in a healthy partnership, both individuals take responsibility for conflict. There is a shared sense of pain. Pain is no one's fault. It is simply an indicator that something in the relationship needs attention. Rather than avoid a fight or a conflict, healthy partners face the issue, knowing that on the other side of the pain comes a new, deeper connection. It is through the resolution of conflict that couples keep passion alive.

Barbara

When Brad and I were having trouble being sexual together, I realized that I was hiding a lot of anger and pain. I was mad at him for career choices he was making, but I wasn't telling him about it. I was also carrying pain and anger meant for my mother and father, but directing it at Brad by withdrawing from him. After I realized these issues, I shared them with Brad. The air cleared. And desire returned. I wanted him again.

Maria

When Graham and I were first married, we had difficulty fighting. We triggered each other with our reactions to conflict. He thought that if we had a fight, it meant something was really wrong with one of us, or with our marriage, so he avoided anger or honesty. I took his avoidance personally, and grew more insistent about a particular issue. I have learned to keep a calm tone when we fight. I sometimes panic when I'm angry. Then my voice gets shrill and he retreats. Not a good combination. We kind of chuckle about this now, but it wasn't funny at the time.

Anger and conflict often bring confusion. Do I say something to my partner? Or do I write about it and share with my therapist? How do I know when to bring something to the relationship? These questions are a healthy indicator that you are learning to live with anger and manage it appropriately. You will make mistakes along the way.

Heather

I remember one night...I was so angry with my husband, and convinced that talking about it with him would do no good. I called a friend in recovery and told her I thought a divorce was the only way through this conflict. She reminded me that perhaps if my emotional reaction was over a "three," I might be reacting to childhood issues. I was definitely over a three...I felt at a ten!

Heather's experience is a helpful reminder that there are times it's better to share angry feelings with a recovery friend, a sponsor or your therapist before you talk with your partner. When the intensity of the feelings have passed, the truth can emerge. The core issue is most likely valid. You will need to discuss it with your partner. But when the emotional intensity exceeds a three on the anger scale of one to ten, it's difficult to have a productive fight. Congratulate yourself for feeling the anger, learning from it, and being willing to be vulnerable with your partner. In the past, you may have sexualized your anger with a secret.

Maria

Early in our marriage, I struggled when I felt too vulnerable. If Graham withdrew from me, I desperately wanted to even the playing field with a sexual secret. But I couldn't. My recovery was strong. It felt gross to resort to those strategies. But I still wanted them when I got really mad.

Maria's experience points to the longing for power that comes in a conflict. If your partner uses withdrawal, either sexually or physically, to cope with anger, you will feel powerless on the other end of him or her. Withdrawing affection or attention is one of the cruelest demonstrations of anger. It may appear benign, but it is a passive way to tell your partner to go away. Maria's urge to have a sexual secret makes sense; how else could she cope with Graham's avoidance? But by staying sober, she learned to sit with the painful feelings–and tolerate them. She gained strength. And she confronted Graham. Now, six years into the marriage, he no longer avoids her during a conflict. In fact, he is learning to be honest with Maria.

Graham was upset with me last week, and rather than get busy or find something to do, he came to me, sat on the bed and asked if we could talk. It was wonderful. He takes risks like this more often, and so do I. We are growing up.

Barbara, Maria, and Heather have used various resources to support their relationships: couples therapy, RCA, weekend workshops with marriage experts, treatment centers and regular 12-step meetings. Their willingness to treat their individual addictions, confront themselves and tell their partners the truth keeps them fit for intimacy. Schnarch calls intimacy the "two-prong process of confronting yourself and self-disclosing to your partner."[28]

During conflict, you are called to know your own needs, desires, and limits and share them with your partner. You reveal your darkness and your light. You share with the intention only to be known and therefore grow closer to your partner. If you have a different reason for telling the truth, you are at risk for manipulating him or her. You cannot always share with a specific outcome in mind. Rather, you share so that your partner can see you and together you can find a solution to the problem.

Committing to Love

Recovery is a continuing commitment you make to yourself. It's a journey of growth as you learn healthy self-care, self-acceptance, and self-love. Each time you take a step to better nurture yourself, you validate that you are worthy of love. And each time you experience a moment of self-acceptance, you heal negative beliefs. As your brain heals, so does your heart. Self-love flourishes from your continued efforts. These three abilities are the foundation for commitment to your work, your home, your pet(s), your friends, your family, and your romantic partner(s). Beware of thinking that can deter your recovery efforts. Expect it. Prepare for it. The addict part of your personality will not appreciate what you are trying to accomplish in recovery. It doesn't want to die. It will try to win and seduce you back into its false promises of bliss and euphoria. Or at least oblivion. Watch for thoughts such as these:

- No one will ever love me if I'm in recovery from love and sex addiction.
- Recovery may work for other people, but it won't work for me.
- I'm not strong enough to face this addiction.
- It seems like everyone is addicted to something so why am I trying to be different?
- This takes too long and what will I have at the end?

As you heal your addiction, you learn healthy ways to protect your heart. You avoid situations and people that put you at risk for fantasy thinking. You watch for impaired thinking by reading recovery literature. Learning to protect yourself from this disease teaches you to honor yourself and your desires. In this way, recovery from love and sex addiction prepares you to be a better guardian of someone else's heart. Maria explains how recovery has made her a better mother. "As I let go of my pain, I have more energy to be a mother." She adds that the birth of her child changed her life.

Before my child's birth, I was completely self-absorbed. I didn't realize this. It was normal for me. But giving birth woke me up. It was the greatest spiritual moment of my life until I discovered the daily spiritual awakenings that come in recovery.

Recovery has given Maria skills as a parent that she would not have had otherwise.

I don't want to be abusive like my parents. But often, I don't know what to do. I read a lot of books. I talk with my therapist, who has her own kids. I am grateful to my friends in recovery who have already raised their children. They teach me and I learn from their mistakes and successes. I feel blessed to be the mother of a teenager who seems secure with himself and generally happy with his life.

Like Maria, Heather has discovered the spiritual opportunity that comes from mothering. She shares the plans she has for her one-year-old son.

I feel tremendous gratitude that I had the gift of recovery before I had a child. I am able to bring an intimacy, an awareness of my child, seeing his personhood, acceptance of who he is, awareness of my reactions to him and tools to deal with the things I was not given in my childhood. I do not want to contribute to a nation of addicts. I want to help my child grow up and know he is worthy of love and is loved simply because he exists. I want to help mold a good person who has the capability to make his own decisions based on what's right for him and not on a driving emptiness to get someone else's approval and love.

As your recovery deepens, so does your capacity for intimacy. You no longer seek to avoid pain, pleasure, or reality. Efforts to manipulate the people you love become distasteful. As you shed the trappings of your disease, the former haze covering your days with a dark cloud lifts and clears. You no longer wake up with dread and anxiety. Instead, you greet a new morning with anticipation and excitement, knowing that blessings are in store for you. You find joy in loving others and contributing to their well-being. Simple tasks bring you pleasure and satisfaction. Self-pity and despair cease to be your constant companions, replaced by the peace of self-acceptance and love.

You become human—complete with imperfections, vulnerability, and beauty. In this way, the sexual healing journey is a beginning rather than a destination. Recovery prepares you for a new life. This new way of living won't always be easy. Sometimes you might feel as if you've made no progress at all. You may find yourself wanting to give up and return to familiar ways of thinking or acting. But when you have lifted some of the pain and shame of your addiction, it ceases to be attractive. You know too much. There is a better way to live. You have seen it in others, and sometimes in yourself. Although the life you want may still feel incomplete or illusive, you are truly ready to heal. Healing this addiction restores the capacity to be intimate. In this way, sex and love addiction brings you a gift: a pathway back to love.

The Twelve Steps of SLAA

Step One: We admitted we were powerless over sex and love addiction–that our lives had become unmanageable.

Step Two: Came to believe that a Power greater than ourselves could restore us to sanity.

Step Three: Made a decision to turn our will and our lives over to the care of God as we understood God.

Step Four: Made a searching and fearless moral inventory of ourselves.

Step Five: Admitted to God, to ourselves, and to another human being the exact nature of our wrongs.

Step Six: Were entirely ready to have God remove all these defects of character.

Step Seven: Humbly asked God to remove our shortcomings.

Step Eight: Made a list of all persons we had harmed, and became willing to make amends to them all.

Step Nine: Made direct amends to such people wherever possible, except when to do so would injure them or others.

Step Ten: Continued to take personal inventory, and when we were wrong promptly admitted it.

Step Eleven: Sought through prayer and meditation to improve our conscious contact with a Power greater than ourselves, praying only for knowledge of God's will for us and the power to carry that out.

Step Twelve: Having had a spiritual awakening as the result of these steps, we tried to carry this message to sex and love addicts, and to practice these principles in all areas of our lives.

Resource Guide

The following is a list of recovery fellowships that may be helpful to you in your particular situation.

Co-Dependents of Sex Addicts (COSA)
612-537-6904
www.cosa-recovery.org

National Council for Couple and Family Recovery
314-997-9808

Society for the Advancement of Sexual Health
770-541-9912
www.sash.net

Overeaters Anonymous
www.oa.org

Recovering Couples Anonymous
314-997-9808
www.recovering-couples.org

S-Anon (for partners of sex addicts)
615-833-3152
www.sanon.org

Sex and Love Addicts Anonymous
210-828-7900
www.slaafws.org

Sex Addicts Anonymous
713-869-4902
www.sexaa.org

Sexual Addiction Resources/
Dr. Patrick Carnes
www.sexhelp.com

Sexual Compulsives Anonymous
310-859-5585
www.sca-recovery.org

Sexaholics Anonymous
866-424-8777
www.sa.org

Survivors of Incest Anonymous
410-282-3400
www.siawso.org

Adult Children of Alcoholics
310-534-1815
www.adultchildren.org

Al-Anon
800-344-2666
www.al-anon-alateen.org

Alcoholics Anonymous
212-870-3400
www.aa.org

Co-Dependents Anonymous
602-277-7991
www.codependents.org

Cocaine Anonymous
800-347-8998
www.ca.org

CoAnon
www.co-anon.org

Debtors Anonymous
781-453-2743
www.debtorsanonymous.org

Narcotics Anonymous
818-773-9999
www.na.org

Recommended Reading

Sexuality and Relationships

*Passionate Marriage: Love, Sex, and Intimacy in
Emotionally Committed Relationships*
David Schnarch, Ph.D.

Open Hearts
Mark Laaser, Deborah Laaser, and Patrick J. Carnes, Ph.D.

The Sexual Healing Journey: A Guide for Survivors of Sexual Abuse
Wendy Maltz

*The Emotional Incest Syndrome: What to do When a Parent's Love
Rules Your Life*
Dr. Patricia Love and Jo Robinson

Stage II Relationships: Love Beyond Addiction
Ernie Larson

Enchanted Love: The Mystical Power of Intimate Relationships
Marianne Williamson

*The Five Love Languages: How to Express Heartfelt Commitment
to Your Mate*
Gary Chapman

Health

*Women's Bodies, Women's Wisdom: Creating Physical and Emotional
Health and Healing*
Dr. Christiane Northrup

Incest and Sexuality: A Guide to Understanding and Healing
Wendy Maltz and Beverly Holman

Prescription for Nutritional Healing
James Balch, M.D. and Phyllis Balch, CNC.

Culture

Of Woman Born: Motherhood as Experience and Institution
Adrienne Rich, Ph.D.

In a Different Voice: Psychological Theory and Women's Development
Carol Gilligan, Ph.D.

Toward a New Psychology of Women
Jean Baker Miller, M.D.

Reviving Ophelia: Saving the Selves of Adolescent Girls
Dr. Mary Pipher and Ruth Ross

Mothering and Friendship

Mother-Daughter Wisdom: Understanding the Crucial Link Between Mothers, Daughters, and Health
Dr. Christiane Northrup

In the Company of Women: Deepening Our Relationships with the Important Women in Our Lives
Dr. Brenda Hunter

The Baby Book
William Sears, M.D., and Martha Sears

Inspiration, Meditation, and Recovery

Living in Process: Basic Truths for Living the Path of the Soul
Anne Wilson Shaef

Legacy of the Heart: The Spiritual Advantage of a Painful Childhood
Wayne Muller

Sabbath: Finding Rest, Renewal, and Delight in Our Busy Lives
Wayne Muller

The Artist's Way: A Spiritual Path to Higher Creativity
Julia Cameron

The Language of Letting Go
Melody Beattie

Radical Acceptance: Embracing Your Life with the Heart of a Buddha
Tara Brach, Ph.D.

Notes

Chapter 1

1. Elizabeth Gilbert, *Eat, Pray, Love* (New York: Penguin Books, 2006).

2. Christiane Northrup, M.D., *Women's Bodies, Women's Wisdom* (New York: Bantam Books, 1994).

3. "Work in Progress: The Relational Model of Women's Psychological Development: Implications for Substance Abuse." Stone Center, Wellesley College, No. 91, 2000.

4. Anne Wilson Schaef, *Escape from Intimacy* (New York: Harper Collins, 1989).

5, 6. Anne Wilson Schaef, *Escape from Intimacy* (New York: Harper Collins, 1989), 75.

7. Anne Wilson Schaef, *Escape from Intimacy* (New York: Harper Collins, 1989), 11.

8, 9. Pia Mellody, *Facing Love Addiction* (New York: Harper Collins, 1992), 21.

10. St. Augustine Fellowship, *Sex and Love Addicts Anonymous* (Boston: 1986), Introduction.

Chapter 2

1. Christiane Northrup, M.D., *Women's Bodies, Women's Wisdom* (New York: Bantam Books, 1994).

2. Christiane Northrup, M.D., *Women's Bodies, Women's Wisdom* (New York: Bantam Books, 1994), 3.

3. Patrick J. Carnes, Ph.D., *Out of the Shadows* (Minnesota: Hazelden, 2001), 15-20.

4. Patrick J. Carnes, Ph.D., *Facing the Shadow* (Carefree, AZ: Gentle Path Press, 2005).

5. Mary Pipher, Ph.D., *Reviving Ophelia* (New York: Ballantine Books, 1994), 39.

6. Christiane Northrup, M.D., *Women's Bodies, Women's Wisdom* (New York: Bantam Books, 1994).

7. Charlotte Kasl, Ph.D., *Women, Sex and Addiction* (New York: Harper and Row, 1989), 14.

8. Charlotte Kasl, Ph.D., *Women, Sex and Addiction* (New York: Harper and Row, 1989), 9.

9, 10. American Heritage Dictionary (Houghton Mifflin Co. 1982).

Chapter 3

1. Christiane Northrup, M.D., *Women's Bodies, Women's Wisdom* (New York: Bantam Books, 1994).

2, 4. Jean Baker Miller, M.D., and Irene Pierce Stiver, Ph.D., *The Psychiatric Care of Women: A Relational Approach to Understanding Women's Lives and Problems* (Journal article from the Psychiatric Annals), 428.

3. Jean Baker Miller, M.D., Judith Jordan, Ph. D., Alexander G. Kaplan, Ph. D., Irene P. Stiver, Ph. D., Janet L. Surrey, Ph. D. *Some Misconceptions and Reconceptions of a Relational Approach* (Wellesley, MA: The Stone Center, The Working Paper Series, 1991), No. 49.

5. Daniel Siegel, M.D., *The Developing Mind* (New York: Guilford Press, 1999), 85.

6. Dr Lawrence Katz, *Keep your Brain Alive: 83 Neurobic Exercises* (New York: Workman Publishing Company, Inc., 1999), 250.

7. Daniel Siegel, M.D., *The Developing Mind* (New York: Guilford Press, 1999).

8. Patrick J. Carnes, Ph.D., *Facing the Shadow* (Carefree, AZ: Gentle Path Press, 2005).

9. Louis Cozolino Ph.D., *The Neuroscience of Psychotherapy* (New York: WW Norton & Co.).

10. Diagram of the Spiral of Disconnection. (Relational Practice in Action: A Group Manual. Wellesley, MA: Stone Center, No. 6, 2000).

11. Patrick J. Carnes, Ph.D., *Don't Call it Love* (New York: Bantam Books, 1991).

12. Alice Miller, *The Drama of the Gifted Child* (New York: Basic Books Inc, 1981).

13. Kenneth Adams, Ph.D., *Silently Seduced* (Deerfield Beach, FL: Health Communications Inc, 1991).

14. *The Prince of Tides* (Columbia Pictures, 1991.)

15. *The Ballad of Jack and Rose* (IFC Films, 2005)

16. Pia Mellody, *Facing Codependence* (New York: Harper Collins, 1989), 15.

17. Pia Mellody, *Facing Codependence* (New York: Harper Collins, 1989), 14.

18. Patrick J. Carnes, Ph.D., *The Betrayal Bond* (Deerfield Beach, FL: Health Communications, Inc, 1997).

Chapter 4

1. *Sex and Love Addicts Anonymous, 1st Edition* (Boston: St. Augustine Fellowship of Sex and Love Addicts Anonymous, Fellowship-Wide Services, Inc., 1986), 70.

2. Patrick J. Carnes, Ph.D., *Out of the Shadows* (Minnesota: Hazelden, 2001), 15-20.

3, 5. *Sex and Love Addicts Anonymous, 1st Edition* (Boston: St. Augustine Fellowship of Sex and Love Addicts Anonymous, Fellowship-Wide Services, Inc., 1986), 74.

4. American Heritage Dictionary (Houghton Mifflin Co., 1982).

Chapter 5

1. Linda S. Leonard, *Witness to the Fire* (Boston: Shambhala, 1990), 66.

Chapter 6

1. Christiane Northrup, M.D., *Women's Bodies, Women's Wisdom* (New York: Bantam Books, 1994).

2. Cathryn Ramin, *Carved in Sand* (New York: Harper Collins, 2007), 90.

3. Christiane Northrup, M.D., *Women's Bodies, Women's Wisdom* (New York: Bantam Books, 1994), 155.

4. Anne Wilson Schaef, *Escape from Intimacy* (New York: Harper Collins, 1989).

5, 6. Patrick J. Carnes, Ph.D., Joseph Moriarity, *Sexual Anorexia* (Minnesota: Hazelden, 1997), 3.

7. Stephen Karpman, M.D., "The Drama Triangle" (USATAA/ITAA conference lecture, August 11, 2007).

8. National Center for the Victims of Crime (Arlington VA).

9. Dr. David Finkelhor (http://www.unh.edu/frl/finkelhor/).

10. Patrick J. Carnes, Ph.D., *The Betrayal Bond* (Deerfield Beach, FL: Health Communications, Inc , 1997).

11. Charlotte Kasl, Ph.D., *Women, Sex and Addiction* (New York: Harper and Row, 1989), 199.

12. Patrick J. Carnes, Ph.D., *The Betrayal Bond* (Deerfield Beach, FL: Health Communications, Inc, 1997).

Chapter 7

1. Stephanie Covington, *Leaving the Enchanted Forest* (New York: Harper Collins, 1988).

Chapter 8

1. Wendy Maltz, *The Sexual Healing Journey* (New York: MSW Harper Collins, 1991), 27.

2. Irving Yalom, *Existential Psychotherapies* (New York: Basic Books, 1980), 40.

3. Tara Brach, *Radical Acceptance* (New York: Bantam Books, 2003), 37.

4. Tara Brach, *Radical Acceptance* (New York: Bantam Books, 2003), 273.

5. Daniel Amen, M.D., *Making a Good Brain Great* (New York: Three Rivers Press, 2005).

6. Jean Baker Miller, M.D., Irene Pierce Stiver, Ph.D., *The Healing Connection* (Boston: Beacon Press, 1997), 177.

7. American Heritage Dictionary (Houghton Mifflin Co., 1982).

8, 9, 10.Wayne, Muller, *Legacy of the Heart* (New York: Simon and Schuster, 1992), 29.

11. Sharon Salzberg, *Loving Kindness* (Boston: Shambhala, 2002), 44.

12. M.Scott Peck, *The Road Less Traveled* (New York: Simon and Schuster, 1978).

13. Wayne, Muller, *Legacy of the Heart* (New York: Simon and Schuster, 1992), 29.

14. Julia Cameron, *The Artist's Way* (New York: G.P. Putnam's Sons, 1992), 197.

15. Julia Cameron, *The Artist's Way* (New York: G.P. Putnam's Sons, 1992), 193.

16. Julia Cameron, *The Artist's Way* (New York: G.P. Putnam's Sons, 1992), 194.

17. Patrick J. Carnes, Ph.D., Joseph Moriarity, *Sexual Anorexia* (Minnesota: Hazelden, 1997).

18, 19. Gerald Corey, Ph.D., *Theory and Practice of Group Counseling, 5th Edition* (Wadsworth-Thomson Learning, 1981).

Chapter 9

1. Sharon Salzberg, *Loving Kindness* (Boston, London: Shambhala Classics, 2002), 14.

2. David Schnarch, Ph.D., *Passionate Marriage* (New York: Henry Holt and Co., 1997), 117.

3. Melody Beattie, *Language of Letting Go* (Minnesota: Hazelden, 1990).

4. Wayne Muller, *Legacy of the Heart* (New York: Simon and Schuster, 1992), 56.

5. Sharon Salzberg, *Loving Kindness: The Revolutionary Art of Happiness* (Boston, London: Shambhala Classics, 2002).

6. Marianne Williamson, *Illuminata: A Return to Prayer* (New York: Riverhead Books, 1994), 150.

7. Tara Brach, *Radical Acceptance* (New York: Bantam Books, 2003), 201.

8. Brenda Hunter, Ph.D., *In the Company of Women* (Multnomah Books, 1994), 109

9. Adrienne Rich, *Of Woman Born* (W. W. Norton and Co., 1986), 237.

10. Brenda Hunter, Ph.D., *In the Company of Women* (Multnomah Books, 1994), 41.

11. Adrienne Rich, *Of Woman Born* (W. W. Norton and Co., 1986), 243.

12. Adrienne Rich, *Of Woman Born* (W. W. Norton and Co., 1986).

13. Marianne Williamson, *Illuminata: A Return to Prayer* (New York: Riverhead Books, 1994), 150.

14. Marianne Williamson, *Illuminata: A Return to Prayer* (New York: Riverhead Books, 1994).

15. Patrick Carnes, Ph.D., Debra Laaser, Mark Laaser, *Open Hearts* (Carefree: Gentle Path Press, 1999).

16. Janet Geringer Woititz, *Struggle for Intimacy* (Deerfield Beach, FL: Health Communications, Inc., 1990), 36.

17. David Schnarch, Ph.D., *Passionate Marriage* (New York: Henry Holt and Co., 1997), 100.

18. Marianne Williamson, *Enchanted Love* (New York: Simon and Schuster, 1999).

19, 20. Charlotte Kasl, Ph.D., *Women, Sex and Addiction* (New York: Harper and Row, 1989), 115.

21. Gary Chapman, *The Five Love Languages* (Chicago: Northfield Publishing, 1992), 35.

22. Gary Chapman, *The Five Love Languages* (Chicago: Northfield Publishing, 1992), 59.

23. David Schnarch, Ph.D., *Passionate Marriage* (New York: Henry Holt and Co., 1997), 113.

24. David Schnarch, Ph.D., *Passionate Marriage* (New York: Henry Holt and Co., 1997), 76.

25. Marianne Williamson, *Illuminata: A Return to Prayer* (New York: Riverhead Books, 1994), 150.

26. Janet Geringer Woititz, *Struggle for Intimacy* (Deerfield Beach, FL: Health Communications, Inc., 1990).

27. *Alcoholics Anonymous - Big Book* (New York: Alcoholics Anonymous World Services, 3rd Ed., 1939).

28. David Schnarch, Ph.D., *Passionate Marriage* (New York: Henry Holt and Co., 1997). 106.

Also:
Sex and the City (HBO, 1998-2004).

Acknowledgements

First, I would like to thank author and therapist Dr. Patrick Carnes for his foundational work in the field of sexual addiction. Without his courage, resilience, research, and vision, this book would not be a possibility. Further, I am especially grateful for the remarkable contributions that Dr. Jean Baker Miller made to the understanding of relationships, women, and power. Dr. Miller passed away in 2006, but her work continues to birth new hope for the field of psychology.

I am also indebted to the wonderful women who agreed to share themselves for this book. They are my personal inspiration and blessing. By sharing their stories of pain and recovery, they make possible a map for other women embracing this journey; the healing of damaged dreams, intimacy, and sexuality.

Books are not born in isolation. I am particularly grateful for the support of colleague Sarah Boggs. She first came to me with a push to write this book. As a well-seasoned therapist from Northern California, her opinions and feedback were critical to the writing process. She listened to me organize chapters and envision the intricate mixture of stories and theory. She edited. Her steady strength took the form of travel as she came to San Antonio and Arizona to be with me. When I felt overwhelmed, she reminded me of the importance of this work. At times, she reminded me of the importance of taking a coffee break. She never wavered in her conviction about my ability as an author and as a therapist. I am eternally grateful for her ability to accompany me into the solitary world of writing.

I am forever indebted to my colleague and mentor, Dr. Lisa Chatillon, whose steady strength and support lays the foundation for who I am as a woman, a therapist, a mother, and a wife. To my dear friend Kara McGinnis whose editing, respect, humor, and trust carried me through times of self-doubt. And to Amy Campbell, a patient editor whose steady work I so much appreciate. Thank you to Suzanne O'Connor for endorsing this project.

I am honored to have the support of two special men in my life. My teenage son, whose merging personhood inspires me each day. And my husband who sustains me with his steady, quiet love. Thank you for saving my place in your hearts while enduring my times of emotional, spiritual, and physical absence.

About the Author

Kelly McDaniel, LPC, NCC, CSAT, is a therapist, public speaker, and graduate of both Georgetown University and St. Mary's University. She speaks regularly about cultural issues that affect women and men. As a certified sexual addiction therapist, she has designed the *Relational Restoration Program* in San Antonio, Texas, where she lives with her family.